Easy
ENTERTAINING

Publications International, Ltd.

Let's get social!

@Publications_International

@PublicationsInternational

www.pilbooks.com

Table of
CONTENTS

BRUNCHTIME FAVORITES

EGGS BENEDICT CUPS

Makes 6 cups

6 **English muffin tops**

6 **thin slices Canadian bacon**

6 **whole eggs**

Salt and black pepper

3 **egg yolks**

¼ **cup water**

2 **tablespoons lemon juice**

½ **cup (1 stick) cold butter, cut into 8 pieces**

¼ **teaspoon salt**

1 Preheat oven to 350°F. Spray six jumbo (3½-inch) muffin cups with nonstick cooking spray.*

2 Press English muffins into prepared cups. Top with Canadian bacon, pressing down into muffins as much as possible. Crack 1 egg into each cup. Sprinkle with salt and pepper.

3 Bake 10 to 12 minutes or until eggs reach desired doneness (egg whites may not look completely set). Remove from pan to serving plates.

4 Meanwhile, combine egg yolks, water and lemon juice in small saucepan; cook over low heat 4 minutes or until mixture begins to bubble around edges, whisking constantly. Whisk in butter, 1 piece at a time, until butter is melted and sauce has thickened. (Do not allow sauce to boil.) Whisk in ¼ teaspoon salt. Serve hollandaise sauce immediately with egg cups.

If you don't have jumbo-size muffin cups, standard (2½-inch) muffin cups can be used instead. Prepare as directed—the ingredients will fit into the cups but it is a much tighter fit.

RICH AND GOOEY CINNAMON BUNS

Makes 12 buns

Dough

- 1 package (¼ ounce) active dry yeast
- 1 cup warm milk (110°F)
- 2 eggs, beaten
- ½ cup granulated sugar
- ¼ cup (½ stick) butter, softened
- 1 teaspoon salt
- 4 to 4¼ cups all-purpose flour

Filling

- 1 cup packed brown sugar
- 3 tablespoons ground cinnamon
  Pinch salt
- 6 tablespoons (¾ stick) butter, softened

Icing

- 1½ cups powdered sugar
- 3 ounces cream cheese, softened
- ¼ cup (½ stick) butter, softened
- ½ teaspoon vanilla
  Pinch salt

1 Dissolve yeast in warm milk in large bowl of electric stand mixer. Add eggs, granulated sugar, ¼ cup butter and 1 teaspoon salt; beat at medium speed until well blended. Add 4 cups flour; beat at low speed until dough begins to come together. Knead dough with dough hook at low speed 5 minutes or until dough is smooth, elastic and slightly sticky. Add additional flour, 1 tablespoon at a time, if necessary to prevent sticking.

2 Shape dough into a ball. Place in large greased bowl; turn to grease top. Cover and let rise in warm place 1 hour or until doubled in size. Meanwhile, for filling, combine brown sugar, cinnamon and pinch of salt in small bowl; mix well.

3 Spray 13×9-inch baking pan with nonstick cooking spray. Roll out dough into 18×14-inch rectangle on floured surface. Spread 6 tablespoons butter evenly over dough; top with cinnamon-sugar mixture. Beginning with long side, roll up dough tightly jelly-roll style; pinch seam to seal. Cut log crosswise into 12 slices; place slices cut sides up in prepared pan. Cover and let rise in warm place 30 minutes or until almost doubled in size. Preheat oven to 350°F.

4 Bake 20 to 25 minutes or until golden brown. Meanwhile, for icing, combine powdered sugar, cream cheese, ¼ cup butter, vanilla and pinch of salt in medium bowl; beat with electric mixer at medium speed 2 minutes or until smooth and creamy. Spread icing generously over warm cinnamon buns.

MAPLE BACON MONKEY BREAD

Makes 12 servings

10 slices bacon, cooked and coarsely chopped (about 12 ounces)

⅓ cup packed brown sugar

¼ teaspoon black pepper

3 tablespoons butter

3 tablespoons maple syrup

1 loaf (1 pound) frozen bread dough, thawed according to package directions

1 Spray 12-cup (10-inch) bundt pan with nonstick cooking spray.

2 Combine bacon, brown sugar and pepper in large bowl. Combine butter and maple syrup in medium microwavable bowl; microwave on HIGH 30 seconds. Stir mixture; microwave 20 seconds or until butter is melted.

3 Roll 1-inch pieces of dough into balls. Dip balls in butter mixture; roll in bacon mixture to coat. Layer in prepared pan. Reheat any remaining butter mixture, if necessary; drizzle over top of dough. Cover and let rise in warm place about 45 minutes or until doubled in size. Preheat oven to 350°F.

4 Bake 30 to 35 minutes or until golden brown. Cool in pan on wire rack 5 minutes. Loosen edge of bread with knife; invert onto serving plate. Serve warm.

CARAMELIZED BACON

Makes 6 servings

12 slices (about 12 ounces) applewood-smoked bacon

½ cup packed brown sugar

2 tablespoons water

¼ to ½ teaspoon ground red pepper

1 Preheat oven to 375°F. Line 15×10-inch rimmed baking sheet with foil. Spray wire rack with nonstick cooking spray; place on prepared baking sheet.

2 Arrange bacon in single layer on prepared wire rack. Combine brown sugar, water and ground red pepper in small bowl; mix well. Brush generously over bacon.

3 Bake 20 to 25 minutes or until bacon is well browned. Immediately remove to serving platter; cool completely.

Note: Bacon can be prepared up to 3 days ahead and stored in the refrigerator between sheets of waxed paper in a resealable food storage bag. Let stand at room temperature at least 30 minutes before serving.

APPLE BERRY CINNAMON ROLL SKILLET COBBLER

Makes 8 servings

- 1 **tablespoon cornstarch**
- 2 **tablespoons lemon juice**
- 5 **apples (about 2 pounds), peeled and cut into ½-inch pieces**
- ½ **cup packed brown sugar**
- ¾ **teaspoon ground cinnamon**
- ⅛ **teaspoon ground ginger**
- 3 **tablespoons butter**
- ½ **cup coarsely chopped pecans**
- 1 **cup fresh blueberries**
- 1 **package (13 ounces) refrigerated flaky cinnamon rolls with icing**

1 Preheat oven to 350°F.

2 Stir cornstarch into lemon juice in small bowl until blended. Combine apples, brown sugar, cinnamon and ginger in large bowl; mix well. Add cornstarch mixture; toss to coat.

3 Melt butter in large (12-inch) cast iron skillet over medium heat. Add apple mixture and pecans; press into single layer to cover bottom of skillet. Sprinkle with blueberries.

4 Bake 20 minutes. Remove skillet from oven. Separate cinnamon rolls; reserve icing. Arrange cinnamon rolls over warm fruit mixture.

5 Bake 20 to 25 minutes or until filling is bubbly and cinnamon rolls are deep golden brown. Drizzle with icing. Let stand 5 minutes before serving.

HEARTY HASH BROWN CASSEROLE

Makes about 16 servings

2 cups sour cream

2 cups (8 ounces) shredded Colby cheese, divided

1 can (10¾ ounces) cream of chicken soup

½ cup (1 stick) butter, melted

1 small onion, finely chopped

¾ teaspoon salt

½ teaspoon black pepper

1 package (30 ounces) frozen shredded hash brown potatoes, thawed

1 Preheat oven to 375°F. Spray 13×9-inch baking dish with nonstick cooking spray.

2 Combine sour cream, 1½ cups cheese, soup, butter, onion, salt and pepper in large bowl; mix well. Add potatoes; stir until well blended. Spread mixture in prepared baking dish. (Do not pack down.) Sprinkle with remaining ½ cup cheese.

3 Bake 45 minutes or until cheese is melted and top of casserole is beginning to brown.

STRAWBERRY CRÊPES
Makes 8 to 10 crêpes

1 cup whipping cream

1 package (16 ounces) frozen sweetened sliced strawberries, thawed, divided

1 package (5 ounces) crêpes (10 crêpes)

1 Beat cream in large chilled bowl with electric mixer at high speed until stiff peaks form.

2 Chop half of strawberries; stir into whipped cream. Spoon about 2 tablespoons of mixture down center of each crêpe and roll up. Cover; refrigerate until ready to serve.

3 Process remaining strawberries in food processor until smooth. Drizzle over crêpes.

PECAN WAFFLES
Makes 8 waffles

2¼ cups all-purpose flour

3 tablespoons sugar

1 tablespoon baking powder

½ teaspoon salt

2 cups milk

2 eggs, beaten

¼ cup vegetable oil

¾ cup chopped pecans, toasted*

Butter and maple syrup

*To toast pecans, cook in medium skillet over medium heat 3 to 4 minutes or until lightly browned, stirring frequently.

1 Preheat classic round waffle iron; grease lightly.

2 Combine flour, sugar, baking powder and salt in large bowl. Whisk milk, eggs and oil in medium bowl until well blended. Add to flour mixture; stir just until blended. Stir in pecans.

3 For each waffle, pour about ½ cup batter into waffle iron. Close lid and bake until steaming stops. Serve with butter and maple syrup.

BREAKFAST SAUSAGE MONKEY MUFFINS

Makes 8 muffins

8 ounces bulk pork sausage

1 egg, beaten

1 cup (4 ounces) shredded Mexican cheese blend, divided

1 package (12 ounces) refrigerated buttermilk biscuits (10 biscuits)

1 Preheat oven to 350°F. Spray 8 standard (2½-inch) muffin cups with nonstick cooking spray.

2 Cook and stir sausage in large skillet over medium-high heat 8 minutes or until no longer pink, breaking apart any large pieces. Spoon sausage and drippings into large bowl; let cool 2 minutes. Add egg; stir until blended. Reserve 2 tablespoons cheese for tops of muffins; stir remaining cheese into sausage mixture.

3 Separate biscuits; cut each biscuit into 6 pieces with scissors. Roll biscuit pieces in sausage mixture to coat; place 7 to 8 biscuit pieces in each muffin cup. Sprinkle with reserved 2 tablespoons cheese.

4 Bake 22 minutes or until golden brown. Remove muffins to paper towel-lined plate. Serve warm.

SPINACH ARTICHOKE EGG SOUFFLÉS
Makes 8 servings

1 **package (about 17 ounces) frozen puff pastry (2 sheets), thawed**

1 **teaspoon olive oil**

¼ **cup chopped onion**

1 **clove garlic, minced**

¼ **cup finely chopped roasted red pepper (1 pepper)**

¼ **cup finely chopped canned artichoke hearts (about 2 medium)**

¼ **cup frozen chopped spinach, thawed and squeezed dry**

3 **eggs, separated**

½ **(8-ounce) package cream cheese, softened**

½ **teaspoon salt**

⅛ **teaspoon black pepper**

4 **tablespoons grated Romano cheese, divided**

1 Preheat oven to 400°F. Spray eight 4-inch or 1-cup ramekins or jumbo (3½-inch) muffin pan cups with nonstick cooking spray. Unfold puff pastry; cut each sheet into quarters. Gently press each pastry square into bottoms and partially up sides of prepared ramekins. (Pastry should not reach tops of ramekins.) Place ramekins on baking sheet; refrigerate while preparing filling.

2 Heat oil in medium skillet over medium heat. Add onion; cook and stir 2 minutes or until softened and lightly browned. Add garlic; cook and stir 30 seconds. Add roasted pepper, artichokes and spinach; cook and stir 2 minutes or until all liquid has evaporated.

3 Whisk egg yolks, cream cheese, salt and black pepper in medium bowl until well blended. Stir in vegetable mixture and 3 tablespoons Romano cheese.

4 Beat egg whites in large bowl with electric mixer at high speed 3 minutes or until stiff peaks form. Fold into vegetable mixture until blended. Divide mixture evenly among pastry-lined ramekins; sprinkle with remaining 1 tablespoon Romano cheese. Fold corners of pastry towards center.

5 Bake 25 minutes or until crust is golden brown and filling is puffed. Cool in ramekins 2 minutes; remove to wire rack. Serve warm.

FRENCH TOAST CASSEROLE
Makes 6 servings

1 **loaf (14 to 16 ounces) day-old cinnamon swirl bread (see Tip)**

4 **ounces cream cheese, cubed**

1½ **cups whole milk**

4 **eggs**

¼ **cup maple syrup, plus additional for serving**

⅛ **teaspoon salt**

1 Spray 1½-quart (6- to 7-inch) baking dish with nonstick cooking spray. Cut bread into 1-inch pieces. (You should have 5 to 6 cups bread cubes.) Place one third of bread in prepared baking dish; top with half of cream cheese cubes. Repeat layers; top with remaining bread.

2 Whisk milk, eggs, ¼ cup maple syrup and salt in medium bowl until well blended. Pour over bread and cream cheese; press gently into liquid. Cover with foil; let stand 30 minutes to 1 hour.

3 Preheat oven to 350°F. Uncover the baking dish.

4 Bake 40 to 50 minutes or until knife inserted into center comes out clean. Cut into wedges; serve warm with additional maple syrup.

Tip: Day-old bread is drier than fresh bread and better able to absorb the custard mixture in casseroles and bread puddings. If you only have fresh bread, bake the bread cubes on a baking sheet in a 350°F oven 7 minutes or until lightly toasted.

BREAKFAST BISCUIT BAKE

Makes 8 servings

8 ounces bacon, chopped

1 small onion, finely chopped

1 clove garlic, minced

¼ teaspoon red pepper flakes

5 eggs

¼ cup milk

½ cup (2 ounces) shredded white Cheddar cheese, divided

¼ teaspoon salt

⅛ teaspoon black pepper

1 package (16 ounces) refrigerated jumbo buttermilk biscuits (8 biscuits)

1 Preheat oven to 425°F. Cook bacon in large cast iron skillet until crisp. Remove to paper towel-lined plate. Drain off and reserve drippings, leaving 1 tablespoon in skillet.

2 Add onion, garlic and red pepper flakes to skillet; cook and stir 8 minutes or until onion is softened. Set aside to cool slightly.

3 Whisk eggs, milk, ¼ cup cheese, salt and black pepper in medium bowl until well blended. Stir in onion mixture.

4 Wipe out any onion mixture remaining in skillet; grease with additional drippings, if necessary. Separate biscuits and arrange in single layer in bottom of skillet. (Bottom of skillet should be completely covered.) Pour egg mixture over biscuits; sprinkle with remaining ¼ cup cheese and cooked bacon.

5 Bake 25 minutes or until puffed and golden brown. Serve warm.

CHEDDAR AND LEEK STRATA
Makes 12 servings

8 **eggs**

2 **cups milk**

½ **cup porter ale or stout**

2 **cloves garlic, minced**

¼ **teaspoon salt**

¼ **teaspoon black pepper**

1 **loaf (16 ounces) sourdough bread, cut into ½-inch cubes**

2 **small leeks, coarsely chopped**

1 **red bell pepper, chopped**

1½ **cups (6 ounces) shredded Swiss cheese**

1½ **cups (6 ounces) shredded sharp Cheddar cheese**

1 Spray 13×9-inch baking dish with nonstick cooking spray. Whisk eggs, milk, ale, garlic, salt and black pepper in large bowl until well blended.

2 Spread half of bread cubes in prepared baking dish; sprinkle with half of leeks and half of bell pepper. Top with ¾ cup Swiss cheese and ¾ cup Cheddar cheese. Repeat layers. Pour egg mixture evenly over top.

3 Cover tightly with plastic wrap or foil. Weigh down top of strata with slightly smaller baking dish. Refrigerate at least 2 hours or overnight.

4 Preheat oven to 350°F. Bake, uncovered, 40 to 45 minutes or until center is set. Serve immediately.

SWEET & SAVORY BREAKFAST MUFFINS

Makes 12 muffins

1¼ cups original pancake and baking mix

1 cup milk

3 egg whites

¼ cup maple syrup

4 small fully cooked breakfast sausage links, diced

1 cup fresh blueberries

1 Preheat oven to 375°F. Spray 12 standard (2½-inch) muffin cups with nonstick cooking spray.

2 Stir pancake mix, milk, egg whites and maple syrup in large bowl until smooth and well blended. Fold in sausage and blueberries. Pour evenly into prepared muffin cups.

3 Bake 18 to 20 minutes or until toothpick inserted into centers comes out clean. Serve warm.

OVERNIGHT BACON, SOURDOUGH, EGG AND CHEESE CASSEROLE

Makes 6 servings

8 slices thick cut bacon, chopped

1 large onion, chopped

1 medium red bell pepper, chopped

1 medium green bell pepper, chopped

2 teaspoons dried oregano

¼ cup sun-dried tomatoes packed in oil, drained and chopped

1 loaf (about 12 ounces) sourdough bread, cut into ¾-inch cubes

1½ cups (6 ounces) shredded sharp Cheddar cheese, divided

10 eggs

1 cup milk

1 teaspoon salt

¾ teaspoon black pepper

Slow Cooker Directions

1 Spray inside of slow cooker with nonstick cooking spray.

2 Heat large skillet over medium heat. Add bacon; cook 7 to 9 minutes or until crisp. Remove bacon to paper-towel lined plate, using slotted spoon. Pour off all but 1 tablespoon of drippings from skillet.

3 Heat same skillet over medium heat. Add onion, bell peppers and oregano; cook 2 to 3 minutes or until onion is softened, stirring occasionally. Stir in sun-dried tomatoes; cook 1 minute. Remove mixture to slow cooker. Stir in bacon, bread and 1 cup cheese.

4 Beat eggs, milk, salt and black pepper in large bowl; pour over bread mixture in slow cooker. Press down on bread to allow bread mixture to absorb egg mixture. Sprinkle remaining ½ cup cheese over top.

5 Cover; cook on LOW 8 to 10 hours or on HIGH 4 to 5 hours. Cut into squares to serve.

QUICK JELLY-FILLED BISCUIT DOUGHNUTS

Makes 10 doughnuts

Vegetable oil for frying

1 **can (about 7 ounces) refrigerated biscuit dough (10 biscuits)**

⅓ **cup coarse sugar**

1 **cup strawberry preserves***

*If preserves are very chunky, process in food processor 10 seconds or press through fine-mesh sieve.

1 Pour about 2 inches of oil into Dutch oven or large heavy saucepan; clip deep-fry or candy thermometer to side of Dutch oven. Heat over medium-high heat to 360° to 370°F.

2 Separate biscuits. Place sugar in medium bowl. Fry biscuits in batches 1 minute per side or until puffed and golden. Remove to wire rack. Immediately toss in sugar to coat.

3 Fit piping bag with medium star tip; fill bag with preserves. Poke hole in side of each doughnut with paring knife; fill with preserves. Serve immediately.

EASY BACON AND EGGS WITH HOMEMADE BAGELS

Makes 8 servings

Easy Bacon and Eggs

1 **pound bacon**

8 **eggs**

4 **tablespoons milk**

Salt and black pepper

2 **ounces cold cream cheese,
   cut into ¼-inch cubes**

Homemade Bagels

2 **cups self-rising flour**

2 **cups plain nonfat Greek yogurt**

2 **eggs, beaten**

**Optional toppings: sesame
   seeds, poppy seeds,
   dried onion flakes and/or
   everything bagel seasoning**

Cream cheese

Fresh berries (optional)

1 For Easy Bacon and Eggs, heat large cast iron skillet over medium-high heat. Add bacon in batches; cook 8 minutes or until crisp. Remove bacon to paper-towel lined plate. Reserve 2 tablespoons drippings. Wipe skillet clean.

2 Whisk 8 eggs, milk, salt and pepper in large bowl. Heat reserved drippings in same skillet over medium heat. Add eggs; cook 3 to 5 minutes or until mixture begins to set, stirring occasionally while scraping bottom of skillet.

3 Gently fold in 2 ounces cream cheese; cook and stir 2 minutes or just until eggs are cooked through but still slightly moist.

4 For Homemade Bagels, preheat oven to 350°F. Spray large baking sheet with nonstick cooking spray.

5 Combine flour and yogurt in bowl of electric stand mixer with dough hook.* Beat 2 to 3 minutes or until mixture is well combined. Place dough on lightly floured surface; knead by hand 4 to 5 minutes or until dough is smooth and elastic. Form dough into a ball.

6 Cut into eight equal portions. Roll each into a ball. Pull and stretch dough to create desired shape, inserting finger into center to create hole. Repeat with remaining dough.

7 Place bagels on prepared baking sheet. Brush with 2 eggs; sprinkle with desired toppings. Bake 20 to 25 minutes or until golden brown. Spread with cream cheese. Serve with berries, if desired.

Or, use heavy spatula in large bowl to combine mixture.

MEDITERRANEAN FRITTATA

Makes 6 servings

Butter, softened

3 tablespoons extra virgin olive oil

1 large onion, chopped

2 cups (8 ounces) sliced mushrooms

6 cloves garlic, sliced

1 teaspoon dried basil

1 medium red bell pepper, chopped

1 package (10 ounces) frozen chopped spinach, thawed and squeezed dry

¼ cup sliced kalamata olives

8 eggs, beaten

4 ounces feta cheese, crumbled

½ teaspoon salt

¼ teaspoon black pepper

Fresh strawberries (optional)

Slow Cooker Directions

1 Coat inside of 5- to 6-quart slow cooker with butter. Heat oil in large skillet over medium-high heat. Add onion, mushrooms, garlic and basil; cook 2 to 3 minutes or until slightly softened, stirring occasionally. Add bell pepper; cook 4 to 5 minutes or until vegetables are tender. Stir in spinach; cook 2 minutes. Stir in olives. Remove onion mixture to slow cooker.

2 Combine eggs, cheese, salt and black pepper in large bowl. Pour over vegetables in slow cooker. Cover; cook on LOW 2½ to 3 hours or on HIGH 1½ to 2 hours or until eggs are set. Cut into wedges. Serve with strawberries, if desired.

APPETIZERS & DRINKS

SPINACH FLORENTINE FLATBREAD

Makes 8 servings

1 tablespoon olive oil

2 cloves garlic, minced

1 package (10 ounces) baby spinach

1 can (about 14 ounces) quartered artichoke hearts, drained and sliced

½ teaspoon salt

¼ teaspoon dried oregano

Pinch black pepper

Pinch red pepper flakes

2 rectangular pizza or flatbread crusts (about 8 ounces each)

1 plum tomato, seeded and diced

2 cups (8 ounces) shredded Monterey Jack cheese

½ cup (2 ounces) shredded Italian cheese blend

Shredded fresh basil leaves (optional)

1 Preheat oven to 425°F.

2 Heat oil in large skillet over medium-high heat. Add garlic; cook and stir 30 seconds. Add half of spinach; cook and stir until slightly wilted. Add additional spinach by handfuls; cook 3 minutes or until completely wilted, stirring occasionally. Remove to medium bowl; stir in artichokes, salt and oregano. Season with black pepper and red pepper flakes.

3 Place pizza crusts on large baking sheet. Spread spinach mixture over crusts; sprinkle with tomato, Monterey Jack cheese and Italian cheese blend.

4 Bake 12 minutes or until cheeses are melted and edges of crusts are browned. Garnish with basil.

Tip: For crispier crusts, bake flatbreads on a preheated pizza stone or directly on the oven rack.

BRANDY COLLINS

Makes 1 serving

2 ounces brandy

1 ounce lemon juice

1 teaspoon powdered sugar

3 ounces chilled club soda

Orange slice and maraschino cherry

Fill cocktail shaker half full with ice; add brandy, lemon juice and powdered sugar. Shake until blended; strain into ice-filled Collins glass. Add club soda; stir until blended. Garnish with orange slice and maraschino cherry.

WHISKEY SMASH

Makes 1 serving

½ ounce Simple Syrup (recipe follows)

2 lemon quarters

8 fresh mint leaves, plus additional for garnish

2 ounces bourbon

1 Prepare Simple Syrup.

2 Muddle lemon quarters, 8 mint leaves and simple syrup in cocktail shaker. Add bourbon; shake until blended. Strain into old fashioned glass filled with crushed ice; garnish with additional mint.

Simple Syrup: Bring 1 cup water to a boil; stir in 1 cup sugar. Reduce heat to low; stir constantly until sugar is dissolved. Cool to room temperature; store syrup in glass jar in refrigerator.

BRANDY COLLINS

PRETZELS 'N SAUSAGE

Makes 12 servings

1 package (16 ounces) hot roll mix, plus ingredients to prepare mix

1 egg

2 teaspoons water

Optional toppings: coarse salt, sesame seeds, poppy seeds, dried oregano

Cooked wheel sausage

Prepared regular or honey mustard

Sliced radishes and fresh parsley (optional)

1 Prepare hot roll mix according to package directions.

2 Preheat oven to 375°F. Spray baking sheets with nonstick cooking spray; set aside.

3 Divide dough equally into 12 pieces; roll each piece with hands to form rope, 7 to 10 inches long. Form into pretzel shape; place on prepared baking sheets.

4 Beat egg and water in small bowl until foamy. Brush onto pretzels; sprinkle each pretzel with desired topping.

5 Bake 15 minutes or until golden brown. Serve warm with sausage and mustard. Garnish with radishes and parsley.

ROBUST CHEDDAR, FETA AND WALNUT CHEESE LOG

Makes 12 servings

8 ounces (2 cups) grated California Cheddar cheese

8 ounces (1 cup) cream cheese

4 ounces (¾ cup) crumbled California feta cheese

2 cloves garlic, minced

¼ teaspoon salt

¼ teaspoon hot pepper sauce

1 cup chopped California walnuts, toasted if desired, divided

2 tablespoons capers, drained

2 tablespoons chopped, roasted and peeled red bell pepper *or* 2 tablespoons chopped pimientos

2 tablespoons gin or vodka (optional)

Pinch cayenne pepper

Combine Cheddar cheese, cream cheese, feta cheese, garlic, salt and pepper sauce; mix until blended and smooth. Add ½ cup walnuts, capers, bell pepper and gin, if desired. Continue to mix until ingredients are incorporated and evenly blended. Mixture will be easier to shape if refrigerated 2 to 3 hours before forming.

Add cayenne pepper to remaining ½ cup walnuts and toss to coat. Spread nuts on sheet of waxed paper.

With damp hands, divide cheese mixture in half. Pat and press each half into ball about 3 inches across or into log about 5 inches long and 2 inches wide. (Shape does not need to be perfect.)

Roll each log or ball in walnuts, patting coating in firmly. Wrap in plastic wrap and chill until ready to serve.

Feta and Fontina Walnut Cheese Ball: Omit the Cheddar and cream cheese and substitute 8 ounces (2 cups) grated California fontina cheese and 4 ounces (1 cup) grated California mozzarella cheese. Combine with the feta cheese and other ingredients as directed above. If desired, roll the balls or logs in a mixture of ¼ cup chopped parsley and ¼ cup dry bread crumbs or rye cracker crumbs.

California Walnut Board

CHEESE BOARD WITH FRUIT, SAUSAGE AND COOKIES

Makes 6 to 8 servings

1 cup (2 sticks) unsalted butter, softened

½ cup powdered sugar

2 tablespoons packed light brown sugar

¼ teaspoon salt

2 cups all-purpose flour

1 cup (about 4 ounces) dark chocolate, cut into small chunks

Honey and prepared balsamic reduction (optional)

Assorted cheeses, sausage slices, proscuitto, crackers and/or pistachio nuts

Assorted fruit such as figs, grapes, prunes and/or blackberries

1 Beat butter, powdered sugar, brown sugar and salt in large bowl with electric mixer at medium speed 2 minutes or until light and fluffy. Add flour, ½ cup at a time, beating well after each addition. Stir in chocolate. Shape dough into 14-inch-long square log. Wrap tightly in plastic wrap; refrigerate 1 hour.

2 Preheat oven to 300°F. Cut logs into ½-inch-thick slices; place on ungreased cookie sheets.

3 Bake 20 to 25 minutes or until lightly browned. Cool on cookie sheets 5 minutes. Remove to wire racks; cool completely.

4 Pour honey and balsamic reduction into small serving bowls; arrange on large serving board. Place cookies, cheese, sausage slices, crackers, pistachios, figs, grapes and blackberries around bowls.

Note: This dough can be stored in the refrigerator for up to 2 days or in the freezer for up to 1 month. Thaw frozen dough in the refrigerator overnight before slicing and baking.

MOJITO
Makes 2 servings

8 fresh mint leaves, plus additional for garnish

2 ounces lime juice

2 teaspoons superfine sugar or powdered sugar

3 ounces light rum

Soda water

2 lime slices (optional)

Combine 4 mint leaves, lime juice and sugar in each of two highball glasses; mash with wooden spoon or muddler. Fill glass with ice. Pour rum over ice; top with soda water. Garnish with lime slices and remaining mint leaves.

COSMOPOLITAN
Makes 1 serving

2 ounces vodka or lemon-flavored vodka

1 ounce triple sec

1 ounce cranberry juice

½ ounce lime juice

Lime wedge (optional)

Fill cocktail shaker half full with ice; add vodka, triple sec and juices. Shake until blended; strain into chilled cocktail glass. Garnish with lime wedge.

MOJITO

ARUGULA-PROSCIUTTO WRAPPED BREADSTICKS WITH GARLIC MUSTARD SAUCE

Makes 16 appetizers

½ cup mayonnaise

6 tablespoons grated Parmesan cheese

2 tablespoons FRENCH'S® Honey Dijon Mustard

1 tablespoon chopped fresh basil

2 teaspoons minced garlic

1 package (4½ ounces) long breadsticks (12 to 16 breadsticks)

1⅓ cups FRENCH'S® French Fried Onions, crushed

½ pound thinly sliced prosciutto or smoked deli ham

1 bunch arugula (about 20 leaves) or green leaf lettuce, washed, drained and stems removed

1 Combine mayonnaise, cheese, mustard, basil and garlic in mixing bowl. Spread half of each breadstick with some of mustard sauce. Roll in French Fried Onions, pressing firmly.

2 Arrange prosciutto slices on flat work surface. Top each slice with leaf of arugula. Place coated end of breadsticks on top; roll up jelly-roll style. Place seam side down on serving platter.

3 Serve wrapped breadsticks with remaining mustard sauce for dipping.

COCKTAIL SHRIMP
Makes 6 servings

1 pound medium raw shrimp, peeled and deveined (with tails on)

¼ teaspoon salt

¼ teaspoon black pepper

¼ teaspoon ground red pepper, divided (optional)

½ cup ketchup

1 to 2 tablespoons prepared horseradish

1½ teaspoons lemon juice

1 teaspoon Worcestershire sauce

⅛ teaspoon hot pepper sauce

Lemon wedges (optional)

1 Heat large skillet over medium heat; spray with nonstick cooking spray. Add shrimp; season with salt, black pepper and ⅛ teaspoon red pepper, if desired; cook and stir 5 to 6 minutes or until shrimp are pink and opaque. Remove from heat; drain well. Cool completely.

2 Stir ketchup, horseradish, lemon juice, Worcestershire sauce, remaining ⅛ teaspoon red pepper, if desired, and hot pepper sauce in small bowl until well blended.

3 Serve shrimp with cocktail sauce and lemon wedges, if desired.

CRAB AND ARTICHOKE STUFFED MUSHROOMS

Makes 30 appetizers

- ½ pound Florida blue crab meat
- 1 (14-ounce) can artichoke hearts, drained and finely chopped
- 1 cup mayonnaise*
- ½ cup grated Parmesan cheese
- ¼ teaspoon lemon pepper seasoning
- ⅛ teaspoon salt
- ⅛ teaspoon cayenne pepper
- 30 large fresh Florida mushrooms

Or, you can substitute mixture of ½ cup mayonnaise and ½ cup plain yogurt.

Remove any pieces of shell or cartilage from crabmeat. Combine crabmeat, artichoke hearts, mayonnaise, Parmesan cheese and seasonings; mix until well blended. Remove stems from mushrooms and fill the caps with crabmeat mixture. Place in a lightly greased, shallow baking dish. Bake in a preheated 400°F oven for 10 minutes or until hot and bubbly.

Florida Department of Agriculture and Consumer Services, Bureau of Seafood and Aquaculture

MOSCOW MULE
Makes 1 serving

½ **lime, cut into 2 wedges**

1½ **ounces vodka**

4 **to 6 ounces chilled ginger beer**

Lime slice and fresh mint sprig

Fill copper mug or Collins glass half full with ice. Squeeze lime juice over ice; drop wedges into mug. Pour vodka over ice; top with beer. Garnish with lime slice and mint.

WHITE SPINACH QUESO
Makes 4 to 6 servings

1 **tablespoon olive oil**

1 **clove garlic, minced**

1 **tablespoon all-purpose flour**

1 **can (12 ounces) evaporated milk**

½ **teaspoon salt**

2 **cups (8 ounces) shredded Monterey Jack cheese, divided**

1 **package (10 ounces) frozen chopped spinach, thawed and squeezed dry**

Optional toppings: pico de gallo, guacamole, chopped fresh cilantro and queso fresco

Tortilla chips

1 Preheat broiler.

2 Heat oil in medium saucepan over medium-low heat. Add garlic; cook and stir 1 minute without browning. Add flour; whisk until smooth. Add evaporated milk in thin, steady stream, whisking constantly. Stir in salt. Cook about 4 minutes or until slightly thickened, whisking frequently. Add 1½ cups Monterey Jack cheese; whisk until smooth. Stir in spinach. Pour into medium cast iron skillet; sprinkle with remaining ½ cup Monterey Jack cheese.

3 Broil 1 minute or until cheese is melted and browned in spots. Top with pico de gallo, guacamole, cilantro and queso fresco. Serve immediately with tortilla chips.

MOSCOW MULE

CHUNKY ISLAND SPREAD
Makes 10 to 12 servings

½ **pkg. (4 oz.) light cream cheese, softened**

½ **cup vanilla lowfat yogurt *or* light sour cream**

1 **can (8 oz.) DOLE® Crushed Pineapple, well-drained**

¼ **cup mango chutney***

Low fat or fat free crackers

*If there are large pieces of fruit in chutney, cut into small pieces.

Beat cream cheese, yogurt, crushed pineapple and chutney in bowl until blended. Cover; chill 1 hour or overnight. Serve with crackers. Refrigerate any leftovers.

BAKED BRIE WITH NUT CRUST
Makes 8 servings

⅓ **cup pecans**

⅓ **cup almonds**

⅓ **cup walnuts**

1 **egg**

1 **tablespoon whipping cream**

1 **round (8 ounces) Brie cheese**

2 **tablespoons raspberry jam**

1 Preheat oven to 350°F. Place nuts in food processor fitted with steel blade; pulse to finely chop. *Do not overprocess.* Remove chopped nuts to shallow dish or pie plate.

2 Combine egg and cream in another shallow dish; whisk until well blended.

3 Dip Brie into egg mixture, then into nut mixture, turning to coat. Press nuts to adhere.

4 Transfer Brie to small baking sheet; spread jam over top. Bake 15 minutes or until cheese is warm and soft.

CHUNKY ISLAND SPREAD

GUACAMOLE
Makes 2 cups

2 large ripe avocados

2 teaspoons fresh lime juice

¼ cup finely chopped red onion

2 tablespoons chopped fresh cilantro

½ jalapeño pepper, finely chopped

½ teaspoon salt

1 Cut avocados in half lengthwise around pits. Remove pits. Scoop avocados into large bowl; sprinkle with lime juice and toss to coat. Mash to desired consistency with fork or potato masher.

2 Add onion, cilantro, jalapeño pepper and ½ teaspoon salt; stir gently until well blended. Taste and add additional salt, if desired.

SALSA
Makes 4½ cups

1 can (28 ounces) whole Italian plum tomatoes, undrained

2 fresh plum tomatoes, seeded and coarsely chopped

2 tablespoons canned diced mild green chiles

1 tablespoon canned diced jalapeño peppers (optional)

1 tablespoon white vinegar

1 clove garlic, minced

1 teaspoon onion powder

1 teaspoon sugar

1 teaspoon ground cumin

½ teaspoon garlic powder

¼ teaspoon salt

Combine tomatoes with juice, fresh tomatoes, green chiles, jalapeño peppers, if desired, vinegar, garlic, onion powder, sugar, cumin, garlic powder and salt in food processor; process until finely chopped.

GUACAMOLE

OLIVE AND CHEESE BOARD

Makes 8 servings

Feta and Olives

- **1 cup assorted olives, pitted**
- **4 ounces feta cheese, cubed**
- **3 tablespoons olive oil**
- **½ teaspoon dried oregano**

Garlic Roasted Olives

- **1 cup assorted olives, pitted**
- **1 celery stalk, cut into 1-inch pieces**
- **2 to 3 tablespoons canned jalapeño pepper slices**
- **1 tablespoon herbes de Provence**
- **1 tablespoon olive oil**
- **2 teaspoons minced garlic**

Garlic Toasts

- **1 loaf French bread, sliced**
  Butter
- **3 tablespoons garlic powder**
- **2 teaspoons dried oregano**
- **1 teaspoon black pepper**
  Assorted cheese, proscuitto, sausage slices, crackers and grapes
  Fresh oregano sprigs (optional)

1. For Feta and Olives, combine 1 cup olives, feta cheese, 3 tablespoons oil and ½ teaspoon dried oregano in small bowl; toss to coat.

2. For Garlic Roasted Olives, preheat oven to 350°F.

3. Combine 1 cup olives, celery, jalapeño peppers, herbs de Provence, 1 tablespoon oil and minced garlic in small bowl; toss to coat. Remove to small baking sheet.

4. Bake 7 to 10 minutes or until lightly browned, stirring occasionally. Leave oven on.

5. For Garlic Toasts, spray large baking sheet with nonstick cooking spray. Spread bread slices with butter; sprinkle evenly with garlic powder, 2 teaspoons dried oregano and black pepper.

6. Bake 30 minutes or until golden brown.

7. Arrange Feta and Olives and Garlic Roasted Olives in serving bowls on board; place cheese, proscuitto, sausage slices, crackers and grapes around bowls. Serve with Garlic Toasts; garnish with oregano sprigs.

JALAPEÑO POPPERS

Makes 20 to 24 poppers

10 to 12 fresh jalapeño peppers*

1 package (8 ounces) cream cheese, softened

1½ cups (6 ounces) shredded Cheddar cheese, divided

2 green onions, finely chopped

½ teaspoon onion powder

¼ teaspoon salt

⅛ teaspoon garlic powder

6 slices bacon, crisp-cooked and finely chopped

2 tablespoons almond flour (optional)

2 tablespoons grated Parmesan or Romano cheese

For large jalapeño peppers, use 10. For small peppers, use 12.

1 Preheat oven to 375°F. Line baking sheet with parchment paper or foil.

2 Cut each jalapeño peppers in half lengthwise; remove ribs and seeds.

3 Combine cream cheese, 1 cup Cheddar cheese, green onions, onion powder, salt and garlic powder in medium bowl. Stir in bacon. Fill each jalapeño half with about 1 tablespoon cheese mixture. Place on prepared baking sheet. Sprinkle with remaining ½ cup Cheddar cheese, almond flour, if desired, and Parmesan cheese.

4 Bake 10 to 12 minutes or until cheeses are melted and jalapeño peppers are slightly softened.

CAULIFLOWER HUMMUS

Makes 3 cups

2½ teaspoons salt, divided

1 head cauliflower, cut into 1-inch florets

½ clove garlic

¾ cup tahini

2 tablespoons lemon juice

Olive oil and paprika for serving

Sliced raw fennel and/or bell pepper strips for dipping

1 Fill large saucepan with 1 inch water. Bring to a simmer over medium-high heat; stir in 2 teaspoons salt. Add cauliflower; reduce heat to medium. Cover and cook 10 minutes or until cauliflower is very tender. Drain and cool slightly.

2 Process cauliflower, garlic and remaining ½ teaspoon salt in food processor 1 minute. Scrape side of bowl. With motor running, add tahini and lemon juice; process 2 minutes or until very smooth and fluffy. Remove hummus to bowl; drizzle with oil and sprinkle with paprika, if desired. Serve with fennel and/or bell pepper strips.

CLASSIC DEVILED EGGS

Makes 12 deviled eggs

6 **eggs**

3 **tablespoons mayonnaise**

½ **teaspoon apple cider vinegar**

½ **teaspoon yellow mustard**

⅛ **teaspoon salt**

Optional toppings: black pepper, paprika, minced fresh chives and/or minced red onion (optional)

1 Bring medium saucepan of water to a boil. Gently add eggs with slotted spoon. Reduce heat to maintain a simmer; cook 12 minutes. Meanwhile, fill medium bowl with cold water and ice cubes. Drain eggs and place in ice water; cool 10 minutes.

2 Carefully peel eggs. Cut eggs in half; place yolks in small bowl. Add mayonnaise, vinegar, mustard and salt; mash until well blended. Spoon mixture into egg whites; garnish with desired toppings.

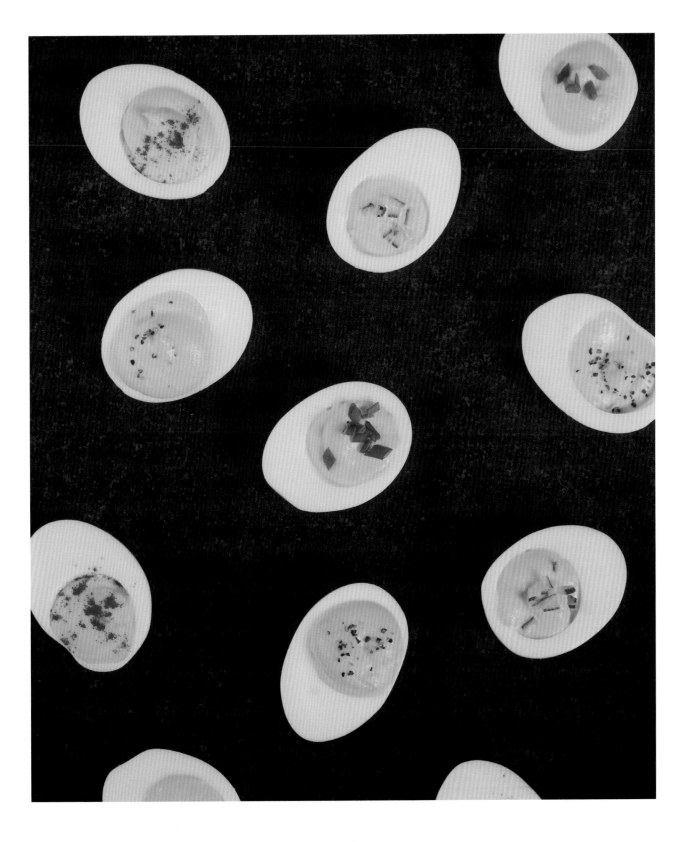

GIN SOUR

Makes 1 serving

2 ounces gin

¾ ounce lemon juice

¾ ounce Simple Syrup (page 42)

Lemon twist

1 Prepare Simple Sugar.

2 Fill cocktail shaker with ice; add gin, lemon juice and simple syrup. Shake until blended; strain into chilled cocktail glass or coupe. Garnish with lemon twist.

Fitzgerald: Add 2 dashes Angostura bitters to cocktail shaker; proceed as directed.

PEPPERONI BREAD

Makes about 6 servings

1 package (about 14 ounces) refrigerated pizza dough

8 slices provolone cheese

20 to 30 slices pepperoni (about half of 6-ounce package)

½ teaspoon Italian seasoning

¾ cup (3 ounces) shredded mozzarella cheese

½ cup grated Parmesan cheese

1 egg, beaten

Marinara sauce, heated

1 Preheat oven to 400°F. Unroll pizza dough on sheet of parchment paper with long side in front of you. Cut off corners of dough to create oval shape.

2 Arrange half of provolone cheese slices over bottom half of oval, cutting to fit as necessary. Top with pepperoni; sprinkle with ¼ teaspoon Italian seasoning. Top with mozzarella cheese, Parmesan cheese and remaining provolone cheese slices; sprinkle with remaining ¼ teaspoon Italian seasoning.

3 Fold top half of dough over filling to create half moon (calzone) shape; press edges with fork or pinch edges to seal. Transfer calzone with parchment paper to large baking sheet; curve slightly into crescent shape. Brush with beaten egg.

4 Bake about 16 minutes or until crust is golden brown. Remove to wire rack to cool slightly. Cut crosswise into slices; serve warm with marinara sauce.

GIN SOUR

BRUSCHETTA

Makes 8 servings

4 plum tomatoes, seeded and diced

½ cup packed fresh basil leaves, finely chopped

5 tablespoons olive oil, divided

2 cloves garlic, minced

2 teaspoons finely chopped oil-packed sun-dried tomatoes

¼ teaspoon salt

⅛ teaspoon black pepper

16 slices Italian bread

2 tablespoons grated Parmesan cheese

1 Combine fresh tomatoes, basil, 3 tablespoons oil, garlic, sun-dried tomatoes, salt and pepper in large bowl; mix well. Let stand at room temperature 1 hour to blend flavors.

2 Preheat oven to 375°F. Place bread on medium baking sheet. Brush remaining 2 tablespoons oil over one side of bread slices; sprinkle with cheese. Bake 6 to 8 minutes or until toasted.

3 Top each bread slice with 1 tablespoon tomato mixture.

GREEN AND RED HUMMUS BOARD
Makes 10 to 12 servings

Spicy Green Hummus

- 1 **can (20 ounces) chickpeas, drained**
- ¾ **cup tahini**
- 2 **jalapeño peppers, seeded**
- ¼ **cup cold water**
- ¼ **cup lemon juice**
- 2 **tablespoons chopped fresh parsley, divided**
- 1 **clove garlic**
- ½ **teaspoon salt**

Red Pepper Hummus

- 1 **can (20 ounces) chickpeas, drained**
- ¾ **cup tahini**
- 2 **red bell peppers, seeded**
- ¼ **cup cold water**
- ¼ **cup lemon juice**
- 2 **tablespoons chopped fresh parsley, divided**
- 1 **clove garlic**
- ½ **teaspoon salt**
- **Olive oil for serving**
- **Walnuts (optional)**
- **Optional dippers: carrot sticks, celery sticks, cucumber slices, pear slices and/or cherry tomatoes**

1 For Spicy Green Hummus, combine 1 can chickpeas, ¾ cup tahini, jalapeño peppers, ¼ cup water, ¼ cup lemon juice, 1 tablespoon parsley, 1 clove garlic and ½ teaspoon salt in food processor; process until desired consistency. Refrigerate. Top with remaining 1 tablespoon parsley and olive oil just before serving.

2 For Red Pepper Hummus, combine 1 can chickpeas, ¾ cup tahini, bell peppers, ¼ cup water, ¼ cup lemon juice, 1 tablespoon parsley, 1 clove garlic and ½ teaspoon salt in food processor; process until desired consistency. Refrigerate. Top with remaining 1 tablespoon parsley, walnuts and olive oil just before serving.

3 Arrange serving bowls of Spicy Green Hummus and Red Pepper Hummus on serving board. Place desired dippers around bowls.

ASIAN SALSA
Makes 4 servings

1 cup diced unpeeled cucumber

½ cup thinly sliced green onions

½ cup chopped red bell pepper

⅓ cup coarsely chopped fresh cilantro

2 tablespoons soy sauce

1 tablespoon rice vinegar

1 clove garlic, minced

½ teaspoon dark sesame oil

¼ teaspoon red pepper flakes

Easy Wonton Chips (recipe follows) and/or assorted fresh vegetables for dipping

1 Prepare Easy Wonton Chips.

2 Combine cucumber, green onions, bell pepper, cilantro, soy sauce, vinegar, garlic, oil and red pepper flakes in medium bowl until well blended.

3 Cover and refrigerate until serving time. Serve salsa with Easy Wonton Chips or assorted fresh vegetables for dipping.

EASY WONTON CHIPS
Makes 2 dozen

1 tablespoon soy sauce

2 teaspoons peanut or vegetable oil

½ teaspoon sugar

¼ teaspoon garlic salt

12 wonton wrappers

1 Preheat oven to 375°F. Combine soy sauce, oil, sugar and garlic salt in small bowl; mix well.

2 Cut each wonton wrapper diagonally in half. Place on 15×10-inch jelly-roll pan coated with nonstick cooking spray. Brush soy sauce mixture lightly over both sides of wrappers.

3 Bake 4 to 6 minutes or until crisp and lightly browned, turning after 3 minutes. Remove to wire rack; cool completely.

ENJOYABLE ENTRÉES

SIMPLE ROASTED CHICKEN

Makes 4 servings

1 whole chicken (about
   4 pounds)

3 tablespoons butter, softened

1½ teaspoons salt

1 teaspoon onion powder

1 teaspoon dried thyme

½ teaspoon garlic powder

½ teaspoon paprika

½ teaspoon black pepper

   Fresh parsley sprigs and
   lemon wedges (optional)

1 Preheat oven to 425°F. Pat chicken dry; place in small baking dish or on baking sheet.

2 Combine butter, salt, onion powder, thyme, garlic powder, paprika and pepper in small microwavable bowl; mash with fork until well blended. Loosen skin on breasts and thighs; spread about one third of butter mixture under skin.

3 Microwave remaining butter mixture until melted. Brush melted butter mixture all over outside of chicken and inside cavity. Tie drumsticks together with kitchen string and tuck wing tips under.

4 Roast 20 minutes. *Reduce oven temperature to 375°F.* Roast 45 to 55 minutes or until chicken is cooked through (165°F), basting once with pan juices during last 10 minutes of cooking time. Remove chicken to large cutting board; tent with foil. Let stand 15 minutes before carving. Garnish with parsley and lemon wedges.

PEPPERED BEEF RIB EYE ROAST

Makes 6 to 8 servings

1½ tablespoons black peppercorns

1 boneless beef rib eye roast
(about 2½ to 3 pounds),
well trimmed

¼ cup Dijon mustard

2 cloves garlic, minced

Sour Cream Sauce
(recipe follows)

1 Prepare grill for indirect cooking over medium heat with drip pan in center.

2 Place peppercorns in small resealable food storage bag. Squeeze out excess air; close bag securely. Pound peppercorns using flat side of meat mallet or rolling pin until cracked.

3 Pat roast dry with paper towels. Combine mustard and garlic in small bowl; spread over roast. Sprinkle with pepper.

4 Place roast on grid directly over drip pan. Grill, covered, 1 hour or until internal temperature reaches 135°F for medium rare or 150°F for medium when tested with meat thermometer inserted into the thickest part of roast. (If using charcoal grill, add 4 to 9 briquettes to both sides of the fire after 45 minutes to maintain medium heat.)

5 Meanwhile, prepare Sour Cream Sauce. Cover; refrigerate until serving.

6 Remove roast to large cutting board; tent with foil. Let stand 10 to 15 minutes before carving. (Internal temperature will continue to rise 5° to 10°F during stand time.) Serve with Sour Cream Sauce.

Sour Cream Sauce: Combine ¾ cup sour cream, 2 tablespoons prepared horseradish, 1 tablespoon balsamic vinegar and ½ teaspoon sugar in small bowl; stir to blend. Makes about 1 cup.

LITTLE ITALY BAKED ZITI

Makes 6 to 8 servings

1 package (16 ounces) uncooked ziti pasta

1 pound bulk mild Italian sausage

3 cloves garlic, minced

¾ cup dry white wine

1 jar (24 ounces) marinara sauce

1 can (about 14 ounces) diced tomatoes

2 tablespoons butter

2 cups (8 ounces) shredded mozzarella cheese, divided

½ cup coarsely chopped fresh basil, plus additional for garnish

¼ cup grated Parmesan cheese

1 Cook pasta in large saucepan of salted boiling water according to package directions until al dente. Drain and return to saucepan; keep warm.

2 Meanwhile, cook sausage in large skillet over medium-high heat 8 minutes or until no longer pink, stirring to break up meat. Add garlic; cook and stir 1 minute. Add wine; cook 4 minutes or until almost evaporated.

3 Stir in marinara sauce, tomatoes and butter; bring to a boil. Reduce heat to medium-low; cook 20 minutes, stirring occasionally. Preheat broiler. Spray 3-quart or 13×9-inch broilerproof baking dish with nonstick cooking spray.

4 Add sauce mixture, 1 cup mozzarella and ½ cup basil to pasta in saucepan; stir gently to coat. Spread in prepared baking dish; sprinkle with remaining 1 cup mozzarella and Parmesan.

5 Broil 2 to 3 minutes or until cheese begins to bubble and turn golden brown. Garnish with additional basil.

TAVERN BURGER
Makes 8 servings

2 **pounds ground beef**

½ **cup ketchup**

¼ **cup packed brown sugar**

¼ **cup yellow mustard**

Hamburger buns

Slow Cooker Directions

1 Brown beef in medium skillet over medium-high heat 6 to 8 minutes, stirring to break up meat. Drain fat. Remove beef to slow cooker.

2 Add ketchup, brown sugar and mustard to slow cooker; mix well. Cover; cook on LOW 4 to 6 hours. Serve on buns.

Variation: For added flavor, add a can of pork and beans to the beef.

BLUE CHEESE STUFFED CHICKEN BREASTS

Makes 8 servings

1 **cup crumbled blue cheese**

4 **tablespoons butter, softened and divided**

1½ **teaspoons dried thyme**

Salt and black pepper

8 **bone-in skin-on chicken breasts**

2 **tablespoons lemon juice**

1 Preheat oven to 400°F. Combine cheese, 2 tablespoons butter and thyme in small bowl; mix well. Season with salt and pepper.

2 Loosen chicken skin by pushing fingers between skin and meat, taking care not to tear skin. Spread cheese mixture under skin; massage skin to spread mixture evenly over chicken breasts. Place in large shallow roasting pan.

3 Melt remaining 2 tablespoons butter in small bowl; stir in lemon juice until blended. Brush mixture over chicken. Sprinkle with salt and pepper.

4 Roast 50 minutes or until chicken is cooked through (165°F).

PICK-YOUR-OWN-TOPPING PIZZA NIGHT

Makes 8 servings

1 package (17.3 ounces) PEPPERIDGE FARM® Puff Pastry Sheets, thawed

Sauces (choose one per pizza):

½ cup PREGO® Traditional Italian Sauce or Marinara Italian Sauce

¼ cup prepared pesto sauce

½ cup prepared Alfredo sauce

Cheese & Toppings (choose one cheese and two to three toppings per pizza):

1 cup shredded mozzarella cheese (about 4 ounces)

1 cup shredded fontina cheese (about 4 ounces)

1 cup shredded Italian cheese blend or 4-cheese pizza cheese blend (about 4 ounces)

1 cup cooked mushrooms

1 cup caramelized onions

¼ cup chopped prosciutto

¼ cup sliced pepperoni

2 tablespoons chopped fresh basil leaves

¼ cup sliced pitted green olives or pitted ripe olives

1 Heat the oven to 400°F.

2 Unfold **1** pastry sheet on a lightly floured surface. Roll the pastry sheet into a 12-inch square. Place the pastry onto a baking sheet. Prick the pastry thoroughly with a fork. Repeat with the remaining pastry sheet.

3 Bake for 15 minutes.

4 Spread the Sauce on each pastry to within ½ inch of the edge. Sprinkle with the *Cheese & Toppings*.

5 Bake for 10 minutes or until the pastries are golden brown and the cheese is melted.

TUNA TOMATO CASSEROLE

Makes 6 servings

2 cans (6 ounces each) tuna, drained and flaked

1 cup mayonnaise

1 onion, finely chopped

¼ teaspoon salt

¼ teaspoon black pepper

1 package (12 ounces) wide egg noodles, uncooked

8 to 10 plum tomatoes, sliced ¼ inch thick

1 cup (4 ounces) shredded Cheddar or mozzarella cheese

1 Preheat oven to 375°F.

2 Combine tuna, mayonnaise, onion, salt and pepper in medium bowl; mix well.

3 Cook noodles according to package directions; drain and return to saucepan. Gently stir in tuna mixture until well blended. Layer half of noodle mixture, half of tomatoes and half of cheese in 13×9-inch baking dish; press down slightly. Repeat layers.

4 Bake 20 minutes or until cheese is melted and casserole is heated through.

BAKED HAM WITH SWEET AND SPICY GLAZE

Makes 8 to 10 servings

1 **(8-pound) bone-in smoked half ham**

¾ **cup packed brown sugar**

⅓ **cup cider vinegar**

¼ **cup golden raisins**

1 **can (8¾ ounces) sliced peaches in heavy syrup, drained, chopped and syrup reserved**

1 **tablespoon cornstarch**

¼ **cup orange juice**

1 **can (8¼ ounces) crushed pineapple in syrup, undrained**

1 **tablespoon grated orange peel**

1 **clove garlic, minced**

½ **teaspoon red pepper flakes**

½ **teaspoon grated fresh ginger**

1 Preheat oven to 325°F. Place ham, fat side up, in roasting pan. Bake 3 hours.

2 Combine brown sugar, vinegar, raisins and peach syrup in medium saucepan. Bring to a boil over high heat. Reduce heat to low; simmer 8 to 10 minutes.

3 Whisk cornstarch into orange juice in small bowl until smooth and well blended. Stir into brown sugar mixture. Stir peaches, pineapple, orange peel, garlic, red pepper flakes and ginger into saucepan; bring to a boil over medium heat. Cook until sauce is thickened, stirring constantly.

4 Remove ham from oven. Generously brush half of glaze over ham; bake 30 minutes or until thermometer inserted into thickest part of ham registers 160°F.

5 Remove ham from oven; brush with remaining glaze. Let stand 20 minutes before slicing.

SLOW COOKER TURKEY BREAST
Makes 6 servings

1 boneless turkey breast
   (about 3 pounds)

Garlic powder

Paprika

Dried parsley flakes

Hot cooked asparagus,
   carrots, roasted onions
   and/or stuffing (optional)

Slow Cooker Directions

1 Place turkey in slow cooker. Season with garlic powder, paprika and parsley flakes. Cover; cook on LOW 6 to 8 hours or until internal temperature reaches 170°F.

2 Remove turkey to large cutting board; cover with foil and let stand 10 to 15 minutes before carving. (Internal temperature will rise 5° to 10°F during stand time.) Serve with asparagus, carrots, onions and stuffing, if desired.

BEST EVER CHILI

Makes 8 servings

1½ pounds ground beef

1 cup chopped onion

2 cans (about 15 ounces each) kidney beans, drained with 1 cup liquid reserved

1½ pounds plum tomatoes, diced

1 can (about 15 ounces) tomato paste

3 to 6 tablespoons chili powder

Sour cream and sliced green onions (optional)

Slow Cooker Directions

1 Brown beef and onion in large skillet over medium-high heat 6 to 8 minutes, stirring to break up meat. Drain fat. Remove to slow cooker.

2 Add beans, bean liquid, tomatoes, tomato paste and chili powder to slow cooker; mix well. Cover; cook on LOW 10 to 12 hours.

3 Top with sour cream and green onions, if desired.

CHICKEN MARSALA
Makes 8 servings

- 8 boneless skinless chicken breasts (6 to 8 ounces each)
- 1 cup all-purpose flour
- 2 teaspoons coarse salt
- ½ teaspoon black pepper
- ¼ cup olive oil
- 6 tablespoons butter, divided
- 4 cups (32 ounces) sliced mushrooms
- 2 shallots, minced (about 4 tablespoons)
- 2 cloves garlic, minced
- 2 cups dry Marsala wine
- 1 cup chicken broth
  Finely chopped fresh parsley

1 Pound chicken to ¼-inch thickness between two sheets of plastic wrap. Combine flour, salt and pepper in shallow dish; mix well. Coat both sides of chicken with flour mixture, shaking off excess.

2 Heat oil and 2 tablespoons butter in large skillet over medium-high heat. Add chicken in single layer; cook 4 minutes per side or until golden brown. Remove to plate; cover loosely with foil to keep warm.

3 Add 2 tablespoons butter, mushrooms and shallot to skillet; cook 10 minutes or until mushrooms are deep golden brown, stirring occasionally. Add garlic; cook and stir 1 minute. Stir in wine and broth; cook 2 minutes, scraping up browned bits from bottom of skillet. Stir in remaining 2 tablespoons butter until melted.

4 Return chicken to skillet; turn to coat with sauce. Cook 2 minutes or until heated through. Sprinkle with parsley.

LAYERED PASTA CASSEROLE

Makes 6 to 8 servings

8 ounces uncooked penne pasta

8 ounces mild Italian sausage, casings removed

8 ounces ground beef

1 jar (about 26 ounces) pasta sauce

1 package (10 ounces) frozen chopped spinach, thawed and squeezed dry

2 cups (8 ounces) shredded mozzarella cheese, divided

1 cup ricotta cheese

½ cup grated Parmesan cheese

1 egg

2 tablespoons chopped fresh basil *or* 2 teaspoons dried basil

1 teaspoon salt

1 Preheat oven to 350°F. Spray 13×9-inch baking dish with nonstick cooking spray. Cook pasta according to package directions; drain. Remove to prepared dish.

2 Brown sausage and beef in large skillet over medium-high heat 6 to 8 minutes, stirring to break up meat. Drain fat. Add pasta sauce; mix well. Add half of meat sauce to pasta; toss to coat.

3 Combine spinach, 1 cup mozzarella cheese, ricotta cheese, Parmesan cheese, egg, basil and salt in medium bowl. Spoon small mounds of spinach mixture over pasta mixture; spread evenly with back of spoon. Top with remaining meat sauce; sprinkle with remaining 1 cup mozzarella cheese.

4 Bake 30 minutes or until heated through.

SESAME HOISIN BEER-CAN CHICKEN

Makes 8 to 10 servings

1 can (12 ounces) beer, divided

½ cup hoisin sauce

2 tablespoons honey

1 tablespoon soy sauce

1 teaspoon chili garlic sauce

½ teaspoon dark sesame oil

1 whole chicken (3½ to 4 pounds)

1 Prepare grill for indirect cooking over medium heat. Combine 2 tablespoons beer, hoisin sauce, honey, soy sauce, chili garlic sauce and oil in small bowl. Gently loosen skin of chicken over breast meat, legs and thighs. Spoon half of hoisin mixture evenly under skin and into cavity. Pour off beer until can is two-thirds full. Hold chicken upright with opening of cavity pointing down. Insert beer can into cavity.

2 Oil grill grid. Stand chicken upright on can over drip pan. Spread legs slightly to help support chicken. Cover; grill 30 minutes. Brush chicken with remaining hoisin mixture. Cover; grill 45 to 60 minutes or until chicken is cooked through (165°F). Use metal tongs to remove chicken and can to large cutting board; let rest, standing up, 5 minutes. Carefully remove can and discard. Carve chicken and serve.

MEXICAN-STYLE SHREDDED BEEF

Makes 6 servings

1 boneless beef chuck shoulder roast (about 3 pounds)

1 tablespoon ground cumin

1 tablespoon ground coriander

1 tablespoon chili powder

1 teaspoon salt

½ teaspoon ground red pepper

1 cup salsa or picante sauce

2 tablespoons water

1 tablespoon cornstarch

Taco shells and/or flour or corn tortillas

Slow Cooker Directions

1 Cut roast in half. Combine cumin, coriander, chili powder, salt and red pepper in small bowl. Rub over roast. Place ¼ cup salsa in 4-quart slow cooker; top with one piece of beef. Layer ¼ cup salsa, remaining beef and ½ cup salsa in slow cooker. Cover; cook on LOW 8 to 10 hours.

2 Remove roast from cooking liquid; cool slightly. Trim and discard fat. Shred meat with two forks.

3 Turn off heat. Let cooking liquid stand 5 minutes to allow fat to rise. Skim off fat. *Turn heat to HIGH.* Blend water and cornstarch in small bowl until smooth. Whisk into liquid in slow cooker. Cook, uncovered, on HIGH 15 minutes or until thickened.

4 Return beef to slow cooker. Cover; cook on HIGH 15 minutes or until heated through. Adjust seasonings. Serve in taco shells. Leftover beef may be refrigerated up to 3 days or frozen up to 3 months.

HONEY LEMON GARLIC CHICKEN

Makes 8 servings

4 lemons

¼ cup (½ stick) butter, melted

¼ cup honey

6 cloves garlic, chopped

4 fresh rosemary sprigs, leaves removed from stems

2 teaspoons coarse salt

1 teaspoon black pepper

16 bone-in skin-on chicken drumsticks (about 3 pounds)

2½ pounds unpeeled small potatoes, cut into halves or quarters

1 Preheat oven to 375°F. Spray 13×9-inch baking pan with nonstick cooking spray. Grate peel and squeeze juice from lemons.

2 Combine lemon peel, lemon juice, butter, honey, garlic, rosemary leaves, salt and pepper in small bowl; mix well. Combine chicken and potatoes in large bowl. Pour butter mixture over chicken mixture; toss to coat. Arrange in single layer in prepared pan.

3 Bake 1 hour or until potatoes are tender and chicken is cooked through (165°F). Cover loosely with foil if chicken skin is becoming too dark.

COUNTRY FRENCH PIZZA

Makes 6 servings

1 tablespoon vegetable oil

1 package SIMPLY POTATOES®
    Diced Potatoes with Onion

½ teaspoon dried basil leaves

1 package (14 ounces) 12-inch
    pre-baked Italian pizza crust

1 cup chopped ham

1 jar (7½ ounces) marinated
    artichokes, drained,
    chopped

1 medium tomato, chopped

1 cup CRYSTAL FARMS®
    Shredded Mozzarella cheese

1 Heat oven to 425°F. In 12-inch nonstick skillet heat oil over medium-high heat. Add **Simply Potatoes®** and basil. Cover; cook 12 to 14 minutes, stirring occasionally, until **Simply Potatoes®** are tender and browned.

2 Place pizza crust on ungreased cookie sheet. Top crust with cooked **Simply Potatoes®**, ham, artichokes, tomatoes and cheese. Bake 10 to 12 minutes or until cheese is melted.

ITALIAN BRIACOLE

Makes 6 servings

2 pounds boneless beef round steak, thinly sliced

2 slices whole grain bread, toasted and crumbled

½ cup chopped onion

¼ cup grated Parmesan cheese

2 cloves garlic

1 teaspoon Italian seasoning

1 egg

3 tablespoons olive oil, divided

½ teaspoon salt

½ teaspoon black pepper

1 jar (24 ounces) tomato basil pasta sauce

Hot cooked pasta (optional)

Chopped fresh Italian parsley (optional)

Slow Cooker Directions

1 Coat inside of slow cooker with nonstick cooking spray. Place round steak on large cutting board. Pound into ¼-inch thickness; cut evenly into two pieces.

2 Combine bread, onion, cheese, garlic, Italian seasoning, egg, 2 tablespoons oil, salt and pepper in food processor or blender; pulse just until mixture is moistened but still chunky. Divide bread mixture evenly over steak pieces; roll tightly to enclose filling. Tie with kitchen string to secure.

3 Heat remaining 1 tablespoon oil in large skillet over medium heat. Add steak rolls; cook and turn 6 minutes or until browned on all sides. Pour ½ cup pasta sauce into bottom of slow cooker; top with steak rolls. Top with remaining pasta sauce.

4 Cover; cook on LOW 4 to 5 hours. Remove steak pieces to large cutting board; cut each piece evenly into seven pieces. Serve over pasta, if desired. Garnish with parsley.

SENSATIONAL SIDES

CINNAMON APPLES

Makes 8 servings

½ cup (1 stick) butter

6 tart red apples such as Gala, Fuji or Honeycrisp (about 3 pounds total), peeled and cut into ½-inch wedges

½ cup packed brown sugar

2 teaspoons ground cinnamon

¼ teaspoon ground nutmeg

¼ teaspoon salt

2 tablespoons cornstarch

1 Melt butter in large skillet over medium-high heat. Add apples; cook 8 minutes or until apples are tender, stirring occasionally.

2 Add brown sugar, cinnamon, nutmeg and salt; cook and stir 1 minute or until glazed. Reduce heat to medium-low. Stir in cornstarch until well blended.

3 Remove from heat; let stand 5 minutes for glaze to thicken. Stir again; serve immediately.

GREEN BEANS WITH GARLIC-CILANTRO BUTTER

Makes 6 servings

1½ **pounds green beans, trimmed**

3 **tablespoons butter**

1 **red bell pepper, cut into thin strips**

½ **sweet onion, halved and thinly sliced**

2 **teaspoons minced garlic**

1 **teaspoon salt**

2 **tablespoons chopped fresh cilantro**

Black pepper

1 Bring large saucepan of salted water to a boil over medium-high heat. Add beans; cook 6 minutes or until tender. Drain beans.

2 Meanwhile, melt butter in large skillet over medium-high heat. Add bell pepper and onion; cook and stir 3 minutes or until vegetables are tender but not browned. Add garlic; cook and stir 30 seconds. Add beans and salt; cook and stir 2 minutes or until beans are heated through and coated with butter. Stir in cilantro; season with black pepper. Serve immediately.

BOURBON PECAN HASSELBACK SWEET POTATOES

Makes 6 servings

6 medium sweet potatoes (about 3 pounds)

1 cup SWANSON® Chicken Broth

¼ cup bourbon

½ cup packed brown sugar

½ teaspoon ground cinnamon

½ teaspoon kosher salt

¼ teaspoon ground black pepper

2 tablespoons butter, melted

½ cup chopped pecans

1 Heat the oven to 425°F. Using a sharp knife, make crosswise cuts into the potatoes (⅛- to ¼-inch apart) almost all the way through but leave the bottoms intact so that the slices stay connected at the bottom. Arrange the potatoes in a 13×9×2-inch baking dish. Fan the slices of the potatoes open slightly.

2 Stir the broth, bourbon, brown sugar, cinnamon, salt and black pepper in a small bowl. Brush the potatoes with the butter, making sure it gets in between the slices. Spoon or brush the bourbon mixture over the potatoes, again making sure it gets in between the slices.

3 Bake for 45 minutes or until the potatoes are tender and the liquid in the bottom of the dish is reduced to about ½ cup. Sprinkle the potatoes with the pecans. Spoon or brush the bourbon mixture from the bottom of the dish over the potatoes.

4 Bake for 5 minutes. Spoon or brush any remaining bourbon mixture from the bottom of the dish over the potatoes just before serving.

GREEK SALAD

Makes 6 servings

Salad

3 medium tomatoes, cut into 8 wedges each and seeds removed

1 green bell pepper, cut into 1-inch pieces

½ English cucumber (8 to 10 inches), quartered lengthwise and sliced crosswise

½ red onion, thinly sliced

½ cup pitted kalamata olives

1 block (8 ounces) feta cheese, cut into ½-inch cubes

Dressing

6 tablespoons extra virgin olive oil

3 tablespoons red wine vinegar

1 to 2 cloves garlic, minced

¾ teaspoon dried oregano

¾ teaspoon salt

¼ teaspoon black pepper

1 Combine tomatoes, bell pepper, cucumber, onion and olives in large bowl. Top with feta.

2 For dressing, whisk oil, vinegar, garlic, oregano, salt and black pepper in small bowl until well blended. Pour over salad; stir gently to coat.

NINE-LAYER SALAD

Makes 7 servings

6 cups baby spinach, packed

1½ cups grape tomatoes

2 cups pattypan squash, halved crosswise

1 cup peas, blanched

4 ounces baby corn, halved lengthwise

2 cups baby carrots, blanched and halved lengthwise

1 cup peppercorn-ranch salad dressing

1 cup (4 ounces) shredded Cheddar cheese

4 slices bacon, crisp-cooked and crumbled

1 Layer spinach, tomatoes, squash, peas, corn and carrots in 4-quart glass bowl. Pour dressing over salad; spread evenly. Top with cheese. Cover and refrigerate 4 hours.

2 Sprinkle with bacon before serving.

CRISPY SMASHED POTATOES

Makes about 6 servings

1 tablespoon plus ½ teaspoon salt, divided

3 pounds unpeeled small red potatoes (2 inches or smaller)

4 tablespoons (½ stick) butter, melted, divided

¼ teaspoon black pepper

½ cup grated Parmesan cheese (optional)

1 Fill large saucepan three-fourths full of water; add 1 tablespoon salt. Bring to a boil over high heat. Add potatoes; boil 20 minutes or until potatoes are tender when pierced with tip of sharp knife. Drain potatoes; set aside until cool enough to handle.

2 Preheat oven to 450°F. Brush large baking sheet with 2 tablespoons butter.

3 Working with one potato at a time, smash with hand or bottom of measuring cup to about ½-inch thickness. Arrange smashed potatoes in single layer on prepared baking sheet. Brush with remaining 2 tablespoons butter; sprinkle with remaining ½ teaspoon salt and pepper.

4 Bake 30 to 40 minutes or until bottoms of potatoes are golden brown. Turn potatoes; bake 10 minutes. Sprinkle with cheese, if desired; bake 5 minutes or until cheese is melted.

HONEY LIME FRUIT TOSS

Makes 7 servings

1 **can (20 oz.) DOLE® Pineapple Chunks**

1 **can (11 or 15 oz.) DOLE® Mandarin Oranges, drained**

1 **large DOLE® Banana, sliced**

1 **DOLE® Kiwi fruit, peeled, halved and sliced**

1 **cup quartered DOLE® Fresh or Frozen Strawberries**

¼ **teaspoon grated lime peel (optional)**

2 **tablespoons fresh lime juice**

1 **tablespoon honey**

- Drain pineapple; reserve ¼ cup juice.

- Combine pineapple chunks, mandarin oranges, banana, kiwi fruit and strawberries in large serving bowl.

- Stir together reserved pineapple juice, lime peel, lime juice and honey in small bowl. Pour over salad; toss to coat.

COUNTRY-STYLE CORN

Makes 6 to 8 servings

4 slices bacon

1 tablespoon all-purpose flour

1 can (about 15 ounces) corn, drained

1 can (about 15 ounces) cream-style corn

1 red bell pepper, diced

½ cup sliced green onions

Salt and black pepper

1 Cook bacon in large skillet over medium heat until crisp; drain on paper towels. Crumble bacon; set aside.

2 Whisk flour into drippings in skillet. Add corn, cream-style corn and bell pepper; bring to a boil. Reduce heat to low. Cook 10 minutes or until thickened.

3 Stir green onions and bacon into corn mixture. Season with salt and black pepper.

ULTRA CREAMY MASHED POTATOES

Makes 6 servings

3½ cups SWANSON® Chicken Broth (Regular, Natural Goodness® or Certified Organic)

5 large potatoes, cut into 1-inch pieces (about 7½ cups)

½ cup light cream

2 tablespoons butter

Generous dash ground black pepper

1 can (14½ ounces) CAMPBELL'S® Turkey Gravy

1 Heat the broth and potatoes in a 3-quart saucepan over medium-high heat to a boil.

2 Reduce the heat to medium. Cover and cook for 10 minutes or until the potatoes are tender. Drain, reserving the broth.

3 Mash the potatoes with ¼ **cup** broth, cream, butter and black pepper. Add additional broth, if needed, until desired consistency. Serve with the gravy.

Ultimate Mashed Potatoes: Stir ½ **cup** sour cream, **3** slices bacon, cooked and crumbled (reserve some for garnish), and ¼ **cup** chopped fresh chives into the hot mashed potatoes. Sprinkle with the reserved bacon.

COUNTRY-STYLE CORN

CHEDDAR BROCCOLI CASSEROLE WITH CRUNCHY TOPPING

Makes 8 servings

1 can (10¾ ounces) condensed cream of mushroom soup

1 cup (4 ounces) shredded Cheddar cheese

2 eggs

¼ cup plain nonfat Greek yogurt

1 teaspoon salt

1 can (5 ounces) sliced water chestnuts, drained

½ cup chopped onion

2 packages (9 ounces each) frozen chopped broccoli, thawed

8 round butter crackers, crushed

2 teaspoons unsalted butter, melted

1 Preheat oven to 350°F. Spray 2-quart casserole with nonstick cooking spray.

2 Combine soup, cheese, eggs, yogurt and salt in large bowl; mix well. Stir in water chestnuts and onion. Fold in broccoli. Pour into prepared casserole.

3 Bake 30 minutes.

4 Meanwhile, combine crackers and butter in small bowl; sprinkle evenly over casserole. Bake 5 minutes or until lightly browned. Let stand 10 minutes before serving.

TRICOLORED PEPPER SALAD
Makes 6 to 8 servings

1 cup diced yellow bell pepper

1 cup diced red bell pepper

1 cup diced green bell pepper

1 cup diced red onion

1 can (15 ounces) ORTEGA®
Black Beans with Jalapeños,
rinsed, drained

¼ cup ORTEGA® Salsa, any variety

1 tablespoon olive oil

Salt and black pepper, to taste

COMBINE bell peppers, onion and beans in large bowl; toss to mix well.

ADD salsa, oil, salt and black pepper; toss to mix well. Chill at least 6 hours to allow flavors to blend.

CHARRED CORN SALAD
Makes 6 servings

3 tablespoons fresh lime juice

½ teaspoon salt

¼ cup extra virgin olive oil

4 to 6 ears corn, husked (enough
to make 3 to 4 cups kernels)

⅔ cup canned black beans, rinsed
and drained

½ cup chopped fresh cilantro

2 teaspoons minced seeded
chipotle pepper (about
1 canned chipotle pepper
in adobo sauce)

1 Whisk lime juice and salt in small bowl. Gradually whisk in oil until well blended. Set aside.

2 Cut corn kernels off cobs. Heat large skillet over medium-high heat. Cook corn in single layer 15 to 17 minutes or until browned and tender, stirring frequently. Transfer to large bowl to cool slightly.

3 Place beans in small microwavable bowl; microwave on HIGH 1 minute or until heated through. Add beans, cilantro and chipotle pepper to corn; mix well. Pour lime juice mixture over corn mixture; stir gently to coat.

TRICOLORED PEPPER SALAD

FRUIT SLAW

Makes 7 cups

1 package (16 ounces) coleslaw mix

1 Granny Smith apple, cut into matchstick-size pieces

1 D'Anjou pear, cut into matchstick-size pieces

1 cup sliced fresh strawberries

⅓ cup lemon juice

2 tablespoons light mayonnaise

1 tablespoon sugar

2 teaspoons poppy seeds

1 teaspoon Dijon mustard

¼ teaspoon salt

1 Combine coleslaw mix, apple, pear and strawberries in large bowl.

2 Whisk lemon juice, mayonnaise, sugar, poppy seeds, mustard and salt in small bowl. Pour dressing over coleslaw mixture; toss gently. Serve immediately.

Tip: To make ahead, prepare salad and dressing and store separately in the refrigerator. Toss immediately before serving.

FRUIT SALAD WITH CHERRY VINAIGRETTE

Makes 8 servings

Cherry Vinaigrette

½ **cup fresh cherries, pitted and chopped**

¼ **cup orange juice**

1 **to 2 tablespoons honey**

1 **tablespoon canola oil**

2 **tablespoons balsamic vinegar**

   Pinch salt

Fruit Salad

3 **cups diced cantaloupe**

1 **large mango, peeled and diced**

¼ **cup sliced almonds**

1 Combine cherries, orange juice, honey, oil, vinegar and salt in small bowl; stir to blend. Set aside.

2 Combine cantaloupe and mango in large bowl. Add dressing just before serving; toss to coat. Sprinkle with almonds.

Tip: For a flavor variation, substitute peaches or nectarines for mango. If fresh cherries aren't available, use frozen cherries, thawed and well drained.

MAMA'S BEST BAKED BEANS

Makes 6 servings

1 bag (1 pound) dried Great Northern beans

1 pound bacon

5 hot dogs, cut into ½-inch pieces

1 cup chopped onion

1 bottle (24 ounces) ketchup

2 cups packed dark brown sugar

Slow Cooker Directions

1 Soak and cook beans according to package directions. Drain and refrigerate until ready to use.

2 Cook bacon in skillet over medium-high heat until crisp. Drain on paper towels. Crumble bacon and set aside. Discard all but 3 tablespoons bacon drippings from skillet. Add hot dogs and onion; cook and stir over medium heat until onion is tender.

3 Combine cooked beans, bacon, hot dog mixture, ketchup and brown sugar in slow cooker. Cover; cook on LOW 2 to 4 hours.

FRUITY WILD RICE SALAD

Makes 6 servings

1¾ cups water

1 package (about 6 ounces) long grain and wild rice mix (fast cook recipe)

½ cup finely chopped dried apricots

⅓ cup coarsely chopped hazelnuts

6 tablespoons chopped fresh Italian parsley

¼ teaspoon curry powder

¼ teaspoon ground cumin

¼ teaspoon black pepper

Pinch ground red pepper

1½ cups finely shredded or chopped red cabbage

1½ tablespoons white wine vinegar

1 tablespoon honey

½ teaspoon salt

1½ tablespoons vegetable oil

1 Combine water, rice mix, apricots, hazelnuts, parsley, curry powder, cumin, black pepper and ground red pepper in large saucepan; stir to blend. Bring to a boil. Cover; reduce heat to low. Simmer 10 minutes or until rice is tender. Remove from heat. Let stand 5 minutes.

2 Remove to large bowl; cool to room temperature. Stir in red cabbage.

3 Combine vinegar, honey and salt in small bowl, stirring until salt dissolves. Whisk in oil. Pour over salad; toss to coat.

LIME & PINEAPPLE SEAFOAM SALAD

Makes 8 to 10 servings

- 2 **cans (8 ounces each) crushed pineapple in juice**
- 1 **package (4-serving size) lime gelatin**
- 1 **cup boiling water**
- ½ **cup cold water**
- 1 **package (8 ounces) cream cheese, softened**
- ¾ **cup coarsely chopped pecans**
- ⅔ **cup celery slices**
- 1½ **cups thawed whipped topping**

1 Drain pineapple in sieve. Squeeze pineapple to remove most of juice. Reserve 3 tablespoons juice.

2 Place gelatin in medium bowl; stir in boiling water until gelatin is dissolved. Stir in cold water and reserved 3 tablespoons pineapple juice.

3 Beat cream cheese in large bowl with electric mixer until smooth. Beat in ¼ cup gelatin mixture until blended. Slowly beat in remaining gelatin mixture. Chill 1 hour or until thickened.

4 Stir in pineapple, pecans and celery. Fold in whipped topping. Pour into clear glass serving dish. Chill 2 hours or until set.

OVEN-ROASTED POTATOES AND ONIONS WITH HERBS

Makes 6 servings

3 pounds unpeeled red potatoes, cut into 1½-inch pieces

1 sweet onion, such as Vidalia or Walla Walla, coarsely chopped

3 tablespoons olive oil

2 tablespoons butter, melted, or bacon drippings

3 cloves garlic, minced

¾ teaspoon salt

¾ teaspoon black pepper

⅓ cup packed chopped mixed fresh herbs, such as basil, chives, parsley, oregano, rosemary leaves, sage, tarragon and thyme

1 Preheat oven to 450°F. Line large baking sheet or shallow roasting pan with foil.

2 Combine potatoes and onion on prepared baking sheet. Combine oil, butter, garlic, salt and pepper in small bowl; mix well. Drizzle over vegetables; toss to coat. Spread in single layer.

3 Roast 30 minutes. Stir vegetables; roast 10 minutes. Add herbs; toss to coat. Roast 10 minutes or until vegetables are tender and browned.

CRANBERRY CRUNCH GELATIN

Makes 8 servings

2 cups boiling water

2 packages (4-serving size each) cherry-flavored gelatin

1 can (16 ounces) whole berry cranberry sauce

1½ cups mini marshmallows

1 cup coarsely chopped walnuts

1 Stir boiling water into gelatin in large bowl 2 minutes or until completely dissolved. Chill 2 hours or until slightly set.

2 Fold cranberry sauce, marshmallows and walnuts into gelatin mixture. Pour into 6-cup gelatin mold. Cover; refrigerate at least 4 hours or until set. Remove from mold.

GRILLED CORN ON THE COB WITH BUTTERY CITRUS SPREAD

Makes 8 servings

8 medium ears corn, husks and silks removed

¼ cup (½ stick) butter

2 tablespoons finely chopped parsley

2 teaspoons grated lemon peel

½ teaspoon black pepper

½ teaspoon paprika

½ teaspoon salt

1 Preheat grill to medium heat. Coat corn with nonstick cooking spray. Grill, covered, 18 to 20 minutes or until golden brown, turning frequently.

2 Meanwhile, combine butter, parsley, lemon peel, pepper, paprika and salt in small bowl; stir to blend. Spread over corn.

SHAREABLE DESSERTS

CHOCOLATE COLA CUPCAKES WITH CHERRIES

Makes 24 cupcakes

1 jar (8 ounces) maraschino
   cherries in syrup

1 package (about 15 ounces)
   dark chocolate cake mix,
   plus ingredients to prepare
   mix

1 can (12 ounces) cola beverage

1 can (21 ounces) cherry pie
   filling, drained

   Cherry Butter Cream
   Frosting (recipe follows)

1 Preheat oven to 350°F. Line 24 standard (2½-inch) muffin cups with paper baking cups.

2 Drain maraschino cherries, reserving syrup. Prepare cake mix according to package directions, using eggs and oil as directed and substituting cola for water. Stir in maraschino cherry syrup and cherry pie filling.

3 Bake according to package directions for cupcakes. Cool in pans 5 minutes; remove to wire racks to cool completely.

4 Prepare Cherry Butter Cream Frosting. Frost cupcakes; top each with maraschino cherry.

Cherry Butter Cream Frosting: Beat 5½ tablespoons butter, softened; 2 tablespoons cream cheese, softened; and 2½ cups powdered sugar in medium bowl with electric mixer at medium speed 1 minute or until fluffy. Beat in 2 tablespoons maraschino cherry syrup until well blended.

ICE CREAM PARTY

Makes about 1½ quarts

2½ **cups half-and-half**

¾ **cup sugar**

1 **cup whipping cream**

2 **teaspoons vanilla**

1½ **cups chopped mix-ins (½ inch or smaller pieces) such as candy bars, toffee, peanut butter cups, chocolate, fresh berries, walnuts, pistachios and/or coconut**

Waffle cones and fresh fruit (optional)

1 Bring 1 cup half-and-half and sugar to a simmer in medium saucepan over medium heat, stirring often to dissolve sugar. Pour into heatproof medium bowl set in larger bowl of iced water. Stir in remaining 1½ cups half-and-half, cream and vanilla.

2 Let stand until chilled, stirring often, adding more ice as needed, about 1 hour. (Cream mixture can be covered and refrigerated overnight.)

3 Freeze mixture in ice cream maker according to manufacturer's directions until soft. Mix in 1½ cups desired mix-ins. Remove ice cream to freezer containers. Freeze until firm, at least 2 hours.

4 Scoop and serve. (This ice cream is best served within 24 hours of churning.) Serve in waffle cones or with fruit, if desired.

Variations: Omit the mix-ins and add ¼ cup chocolate or strawberry syrup to make chocolate and/or strawberry ice cream.

SIMPLY DREAMY CHERRY CHEESECAKE SQUARES

Makes 12 to 14 servings

- 2 **cups graham cracker crumbs**
- ½ **cup (1 stick) butter, melted**
- 2 **cups milk**
- 1 **package (4-serving size) cheesecake instant pudding and pie filling mix**
- 4 **cups frozen whipped topping, divided**
- 1 **can (21 ounces) cherry pie filling**

1 Combine graham cracker crumbs and butter in medium bowl. Press into bottom of 13×9-inch baking pan.

2 Whisk milk into pudding mix in medium bowl until well blended. Fold in 2 cups whipped topping. Spread over crust. Spread pie filling over pudding mixture. Spread remaining 2 cups whipped topping over pie filling.

3 Refrigerate 2 hours or until chilled. Cut into squares.

CHOCOLATE MOUSSE

Makes 6 servings

- 1 **package (12 ounces) semisweet chocolate chips**
- 6 **tablespoons (¾ stick) unsalted butter**
- ¼ **cup brewed strong coffee**
- 3 **eggs, separated**
- ½ **cup whipping cream**
- ¼ **cup superfine sugar**

1 Combine chocolate chips, butter and coffee in large saucepan over low heat; cook and stir until smooth. Whisk in egg yolks, one at a time, until well blended. Remove from heat; cool slightly.

2 Beat cream in small bowl with electric mixer at high speed until soft peaks form. Refrigerate until ready to use.

3 Beat egg whites in medium bowl until soft peaks form. Add sugar, 1 tablespoon at a time. Beat until stiff peaks form and mixture is shiny.

4 Fold egg whites into whipped cream mixture. Fold in cooled chocolate mixture. Cover and chill 4 hours.

SIMPLY DREAMY CHERRY CHEESECAKE SQUARES

REFRIGERATOR COOKIES

Makes about 4 dozen

½ **cup sugar**

¼ **cup light corn syrup**

¼ **cup (½ stick) butter, softened**

1 **egg**

1 **teaspoon vanilla**

1¾ **cups all-purpose flour**

¼ **teaspoon baking soda**

¼ **teaspoon salt**

Decors and decorating sugars (optional)

1 Beat sugar, corn syrup and butter in large bowl. Add egg and vanilla; mix well.

2 Combine flour, baking soda and salt in medium bowl. Add to sugar mixture; mix well. Shape dough into two rolls 1½ inches in diameter. Wrap in plastic wrap. Freeze 1 hour.

3 Preheat oven to 350°F. Line cookie sheets with parchment paper. Cut dough into ¼-inch-thick slices; place 1 inch apart on prepared cookie sheets. Sprinkle with decors, if desired.

4 Bake 8 to 10 minutes or until edges are golden brown. Remove to wire racks; cool completely.

Variations: Add 2 tablespoons unsweetened cocoa powder to dough for chocolate cookies. For sugar-rimmed cookies, roll logs in colored sugar before slicing.

SPICED PEACH PIE

Makes 8 servings

1 package (14 ounces) refrigerated pie crust (2 crusts), divided

1 egg, separated

2 tablespoons cornstarch

2 teaspoons ground cinnamon

½ teaspoon ground nutmeg

¼ teaspoon salt

½ cup unsweetened apple juice concentrate

1 teaspoon vanilla

5 cups sliced peeled fresh peaches *or* frozen unsweetened sliced peaches, thawed and well drained

1 tablespoon butter, cubed or cut into small pieces

1 teaspoon cold water

1 Preheat oven to 400°F. Line 9-inch pie plate with 1 pie crust. Beat egg white in small bowl until frothy; brush over pastry.

2 Combine cornstarch, cinnamon, nutmeg and salt in large bowl; mix well. Stir in juice concentrate and vanilla. Add peaches; toss lightly to coat. Spoon into crust; dot with butter.

3 Cut remaining 1 pie crust into ½-inch-wide strips. Arrange in lattice design over peaches. Seal and flute edge. Whisk egg yolk and cold water in small bowl; brush over pastry.

4 Bake 50 minutes or until pastry is golden brown and filling is thick and bubbly.* Cool on wire rack. Serve warm, at room temperature or chilled.

Cover pie loosely with foil after 30 minutes of baking to prevent overbrowning, if necessary.

CELEBRATION BROWNIES

Makes 2 to 3 dozen

1 cup (2 sticks) butter

8 ounces semisweet baking chocolate, coarsely chopped

1 cup sugar

4 eggs

1 teaspoon vanilla

1 teaspoon salt

1¼ cups all-purpose flour

2 cups dark or semisweet chocolate chips, divided

¼ cup whipping cream

1 container (about 2 ounces) rainbow nonpareils

1 Preheat oven to 350°F. Spray 13×9-inch baking pan with nonstick cooking spray or line with parchment paper.

2 Heat butter and chocolate in large heavy saucepan over low heat; stir until melted and smooth. Remove from heat; stir in sugar until blended. Stir in eggs, one at a time, until well blended after each addition. Stir in vanilla and salt. Add flour and 1 cup chocolate chips; stir just until blended. Spread batter evenly in prepared pan.

3 Bake 22 to 25 minutes or until center is set and toothpick inserted into center comes out clean. Cool completely in pan on wire rack.

4 Heat cream in small saucepan over medium-low heat until bubbles appear around edge of pan. Remove from heat; add remaining 1 cup chocolate chips. Let stand 1 minute; whisk until smooth and well blended. Spread evenly over brownies; top with nonpareils.

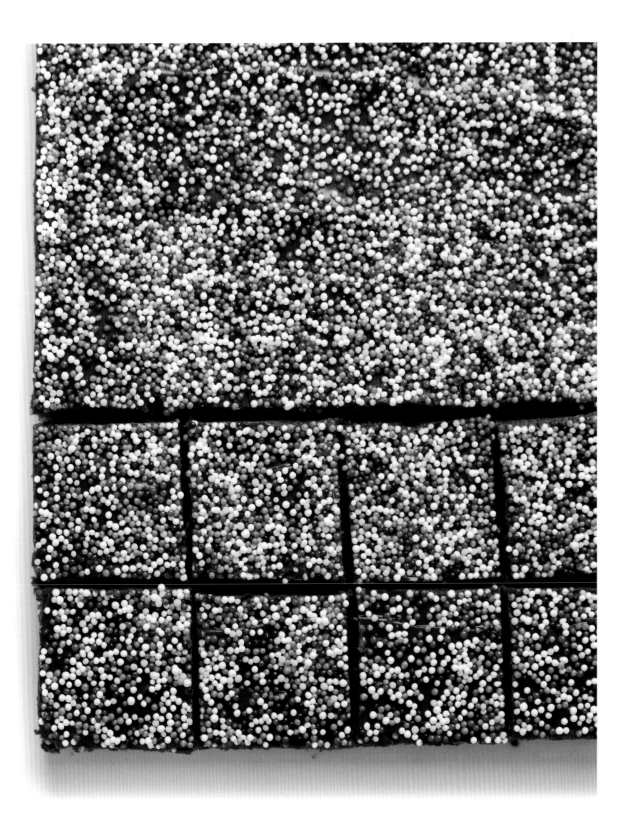

LIME CHIFFON PIE
Makes 6 servings

1 **cup sugar, divided**

1 **envelope (1 tablespoon) unflavored gelatin**

⅛ **teaspoon salt**

1 **cup cola beverage**

3 **eggs, separated**

¼ **cup fresh lime juice**

¼ **cup dark rum *or* 1 tablespoon rum extract**

1 **cup whipped topping or whipped cream**

1 **9-inch graham cracker or chocolate cookie crust or baked pie shell**

2 **tablespoons grated lime peel**

1 Stir together ½ cup sugar, gelatin and salt in top of double boiler. Stir in cola. Whisk egg yolks; stir into gelatin mixture. Cook over boiling water, stirring constantly, until gelatin is dissolved, about 5 minutes.

2 Remove from boiling water; stir in lime juice and rum. Chill until mixture mounds when dropped from spoon. Beat egg whites in large bowl with electric mixer until soft peaks form. Gradually beat in remaining ½ cup sugar, beating until stiff and glossy. Carefully fold gelatin mixture into whipped topping, then fold into egg whites. Chill several minutes before placing into pie crust.

3 Sprinkle pie with grated lime peel. Chill several hours or until firm. If desired, top with dollop of whipped cream.

CHOCOLATE-DIPPED STRAWBERRIES, COOKIES AND CANDY BOARD

Makes 8 servings

Chocolate-Dipped Strawberries

- 2 **cups white chocolate chips, divided**
- 1 **cup semisweet chocolate chips**
- 3 **to 4 drops red food coloring**
- 2 **quarts fresh strawberries**

Cookies

- 1 **package (8 ounces) cream cheese, softened**
- ½ **cup (1 stick) butter, softened**
- 1 **egg**
- 1 **package (about 18 ounces) devil's food cake mix**
- ½ **cup chopped pecans, toasted***
- ½ **cup semisweet chocolate chips**
  Assorted red sugar candies
  Assorted candies and prepared cookies

*To toast pecans, spread in single layer in heavy skillet. Cook and stir over medium heat 1 to 2 minutes or until nuts are lightly browned.

1 For Chocolate-Dipped Strawberries, place 1 cup white chocolate chips in small microwavable bowl. Repeat with remaining 1 cup white chocolate chips and 1 cup semisweet chocolate chips. Microwave each bowl separately on HIGH 2 to 3 minutes or until smooth when stirred, stirring after each minute.

2 Add food coloring to one bowl of white chocolate chips until desired shade of pink is reached. Dip strawberries into melted chocolate mixtures; decorate as desired. Place on waxed paper-lined baking sheet; let stand until chocolate is set.

3 For Cookies, preheat oven to 350°F. Beat cream cheese and butter in medium bowl with electric mixer at low speed 30 seconds or until smooth. Add egg; beat at medium speed until well blended. Add cake mix; beat at low speed 2 minutes or until mixture is smooth. Stir in pecans. Shape dough into 1-inch balls on large ungreased cookie sheets.

4 Bake 8 minutes. (Cookies will appear underbaked.) Cool on cookie sheets 5 minutes. Remove to wire racks.

5 Place ½ cup semisweet chocolate chips in small microwavable bowl. Microwave on HIGH 1 to 2 minutes or until smooth when stirred, stirring after each minute. Spoon small amount of melted chocolate on top of each cookie; attached sugar candy. Let cookies cool completely.

6 Arrange Chocolate-Dipped Strawberries, Cookies, assorted candies and prepared cookies on large serving board.

PINEAPPLE UPSIDE DOWN CAKE

Makes 8 servings

½ cup packed brown sugar

¼ cup (½ stick) butter, melted

1 package (about 15 ounces) yellow cake mix, plus ingredients to prepare mix

1 can (20 ounces) pineapple slices in juice, well drained on paper towels and ½ cup juice reserved

14 to 16 maraschino cherries, stems removed and well drained on paper towels

Slow Cooker Directions

1 Coat inside of slow cooker with nonstick cooking spray.

2 Combine brown sugar and butter in small bowl; stir to blend. Spread brown sugar mixture evenly onto bottom of slow cooker. Place cake mix in large bowl. Reserve two pineapple slices for another use or discard. Place remaining pineapple slices and cherries into cake mix; coat evenly. Arrange pineapple slices on brown sugar mixture; place cherry in center of each. Place remaining cherries in any remaining spaces between pineapple slices.

3 Prepare remaining cake mix as directed on box, substituting ½ cup pineapple juice for the water. Pour batter evenly over pineapple and cherries.

4 Place clean kitchen towel over top of slow cooker. Cover; cook on HIGH 2 hours, 15 minutes or until toothpick inserted into center comes out clean. Remove stoneware to wire rack; cool 10 minutes. Invert stoneware onto large serving plate.

BUTTERSCOTCH BUNDT CAKE

Makes 12 to 16 servings

1 package (about 15 ounces) yellow cake mix

1 package (4-serving size) butterscotch instant pudding and pie filling mix

1 cup water

3 eggs

2 teaspoons ground cinnamon

½ cup chopped pecans

Powdered sugar (optional)

1 Preheat oven to 325°F. Spray 12-cup bundt pan with nonstick cooking spray.

2 Beat cake mix, pudding mix, water, eggs and cinnamon in large bowl with electric mixer at medium speed 2 minutes or until blended. Stir in pecans. Pour batter into prepared pan.

3 Bake 40 to 50 minutes or until cake springs back when lightly touched. Cool in pan on wire rack 10 minutes. Invert cake onto serving plate; cool completely. Sprinkle with powdered sugar, if desired.

Pistachio Walnut Bundt Cake: Substitute white cake mix for yellow cake mix, pistachio pudding mix for butterscotch pudding mix and walnuts for pecans.

STRAWBERRY NAPOLEONS
Makes 9 napoleons

1 **quart fresh strawberries**

1 **sheet (half of 17-ounce package) puff pastry, thawed**

1 **container (8 ounces) whipped topping, thawed**

1 Remove stems from strawberries; slice strawberries into large bowl and set aside until ready to use.

2 Preheat oven to 400°F. Line large baking sheet with parchment paper. Unfold pastry sheet; cut into 3 strips along fold marks. Cut each strip crosswise into thirds, forming 9 squares total. Place pastry squares on prepared baking sheet. Bake 12 to 15 minutes or until puffed and golden brown. Remove to wire rack to cool completely.

3 For each napoleon, split 1 puff pastry square in half horizontally. Place 1 half on serving plate; top with whipped topping and sliced strawberries. Repeat layers.

CHOCOLATE TURTLE CHEESECAKE
Makes 12 servings

24 chocolate sandwich cookies, ground (about 2¾ cups)

2 tablespoons butter, melted

2 packages (8 ounces each) cream cheese, softened

2 eggs

⅓ cup sugar

¼ cup sour cream

1 teaspoon vanilla

½ cup caramel ice cream topping

½ cup hot fudge topping

½ cup pecan halves

1 Preheat oven to 350°F. Combine ground cookies and butter in medium bowl; pat evenly on bottom and 1 inch up side of 9-inch springform pan. Place in freezer while preparing filling.

2 Beat cream cheese in large bowl with electric mixer until fluffy. Beat in eggs, sugar, sour cream and vanilla until smooth. Pour mixture into prepared crust.

3 Bake cheesecake 30 to 35 minutes or until almost set in center. Cool on wire rack. Refrigerate, loosely covered, 8 hours or up to 3 days.

4 Remove side of springform pan from cheesecake; place on serving plate. Drizzle caramel and fudge toppings over cake. Top cheesecake with pecan halves.

CHOCOLATE MOLÉ FONDUE

Makes 6 servings

Cinnamon Chips

- 2 tablespoons granulated sugar
- 2 teaspoons ground cinnamon
- 6 (8-inch) ORTEGA® Flour Soft Tortillas

  Butter-flavored cooking spray

Fondue

- 1 cup semisweet or dark chocolate chips
- ½ cup whipping cream
- 3 tablespoons ORTEGA® Taco Sauce, any variety

PREHEAT oven to 350°F. Combine sugar and cinnamon in small bowl. Set aside.

COAT one side of each tortilla with cooking spray. Cut into wedges; arrange in single layer on large baking sheet, coated side down. Sprinkle evenly with cinnamon-sugar. Spray again with cooking spray.

BAKE 8 to 10 minutes or until crisp, turning once.

COMBINE chocolate chips, whipping cream and taco sauce in small saucepan over low heat. Cook and stir until chocolate has melted and mixture is smooth.

KEEP chocolate mixture warm in small saucepan, slow cooker or fondue pot. Serve with cinnamon chips for dipping.

5-MINUTE TRIFLE

Makes 8 servings

2 packages ladyfingers

¼ cup plus 2 tablespoons sherry or orange liqueur

1 cup raspberry fruit spread or preserves

2 packages (4-serving size) instant vanilla pudding mix

3 cups cold milk

1 cup whipping cream

2 packages (4 ounces) slivered almonds

2 pints fresh raspberries

1 Separate ladyfingers. Sprinkle cut sides with sherry and spread with raspberry spread. Arrange ladyfingers vertically along sides of trifle dish or glass serving bowl with raspberry sides facing in.

2 Combine pudding mix and milk in large bowl; stir until well blended. Fold in cream until well blended. Spoon pudding mixture into center of bowl; top with almonds and berries. Serve immediately or cover and chill.

CAFÉ MOCHA CUPCAKES
Makes 24 servings

2 tablespoons plus 2 teaspoons instant coffee powder, divided

1⅓ cups plus 1 tablespoon water, divided

1 package (about 18 ounces) devil's food cake mix

3 eggs

⅓ cup canola oil

1 container (8 ounces) thawed frozen whipped topping

Cocoa powder (optional)

1 Preheat oven to 350°F. Line 24 standard (2½-inch) muffin cups with paper baking cups.

2 Dissolve 2 tablespoons coffee powder in 1⅓ cups water in large bowl. Add cake mix, eggs and oil; beat with electric mixer at low speed 30 seconds. Beat at medium speed 2 minutes, scraping bowl occasionally. Pour batter evenly into prepared muffin cups.

3 Bake 17 to 22 minutes or until toothpick inserted into centers comes out clean. Remove cupcakes from pan; cool completely on wire rack.

4 Dissolve remaining 2 teaspoons coffee powder in 1 tablespoon water in small cup. Fold coffee mixture into whipped topping until well blended. Spread frosting over cupcakes; sprinkle with cocoa powder, if desired. Serve immediately or cover and refrigerate until ready to serve.

LEMON BLACKBERRY COBBLER

Makes 8 servings

1 package (about 17 ounces) sugar cookie mix

6 tablespoons (¾ stick) butter, softened

1 egg

2 tablespoons all-purpose flour, plus additional for work surface

2 tablespoons grated lemon peel

4 containers (6 ounces each) fresh blackberries

⅓ cup sugar

3 tablespoons lemon juice

3 tablespoons cornstarch

1 Preheat oven to 375°F.

2 Combine cookie mix, butter, egg and 2 tablespoons flour in large bowl; mix well. Divide dough in half; wrap and reserve half for another use. Add lemon peel to remaining dough. Wrap with plastic wrap; refrigerate 30 minutes or until firm.

3 Combine blackberries, sugar, lemon juice and cornstarch in medium bowl; toss gently to coat. Spoon into 9-inch deep-dish pie plate.

4 Roll out dough into 9-inch circle on lightly floured surface; cut into 12 equal strips. Arrange strips in lattice design over blackberries; trim excess dough from edge. (If dough becomes too soft to work with, refrigerate again before doing lattice.)

5 Bake 30 minutes. *Reduce oven temperature to 325°F.* Cover edge of crust with foil if overbrowning. Bake 18 to 20 minutes or until toothpick inserted into center of crust comes out clean. Let stand 15 minutes before serving for filling to set.

REVERSE CHOCOLATE CHIP COOKIES

Makes 3 dozen

- 4 ounces unsweetened chocolate
- 2 cups all-purpose flour
- 1½ teaspoons baking powder
- ½ teaspoon salt
- 1½ cups packed brown sugar
- ¾ cup (1½ sticks) butter, softened
- 1 teaspoon vanilla
- 2 eggs
- 1 package (12 ounces) white chocolate chips

1 Preheat oven to 350°F. Melt unsweetened chocolate according to package directions; cool slightly.

2 Combine flour, baking powder and salt in medium bowl. Beat brown sugar, butter and vanilla in large bowl with electric mixer at medium speed until light and fluffy. Add eggs; beat until well blended. Beat in melted chocolate. Gradually add flour mixture, mixing well after each addition. Stir in white chocolate chips. Drop by heaping tablespoonfuls 2 inches apart onto ungreased cookie sheets.

3 Bake 10 minutes or just until set. Cool on cookie sheets 1 minute. Remove to wire racks; cool completely. Store in tightly covered container up to 1 week.

STRAWBERRY CHEESECAKE DESSERT SHOOTERS

Makes 8 to 10 servings

1 cup graham cracker crumbs, plus additional for garnish

¼ cup (½ stick) butter, melted

2 cups chopped fresh strawberries

¾ cup sugar, divided

12 ounces cream cheese, softened

2 eggs

2 tablespoons sour cream

½ teaspoon vanilla

Whipped cream

1 Place 1 cup graham cracker crumbs in medium nonstick skillet; cook and stir over medium heat 3 minutes or until lightly browned. Remove to small bowl; stir in butter until well blended. Press mixture evenly into 8 to 10 (3- to 4-ounce) shot glasses.

2 Combine strawberries and ¼ cup sugar in small bowl; toss to coat. Cover; refrigerate until ready to serve.

3 Beat cream cheese in medium bowl with electric mixer at medium speed until creamy. Add eggs, remaining ½ cup sugar, sour cream and vanilla; beat until well blended. Remove to medium saucepan; cook and stir over medium heat 5 to 6 minutes or until thickened and smooth. Divide filling evenly among prepared crusts. Refrigerate 1 hour or until cold.

4 Top each serving with strawberries and whipped cream. Garnish with additional graham cracker crumbs.

Tip: For larger servings, use four to five 6- or 8-ounce juice or stemless wine glasses. Divide crumb mixture, filling and strawberries evenly among glasses.

BROWNIE CHEESECAKE
Makes 10 to 12 servings

1 cup ¾-inch brownie pieces (recipe follows)

Chocolate Crumb Crust (recipe follows)

4 packages (8 ounce each) cream cheese, softened

1 cup sugar

1½ teaspoons vanilla extract

4 eggs

1 Prepare brownies using recipe below or your own favorite recipe.

2 Heat oven to 350°F. Prepare Chocolate Crumb Crust; cool slightly. Beat cream cheese, sugar and vanilla until smooth. Gradually add eggs, beating well after each addition. Pour batter into prepared crust.

3 Sprinkle brownie pieces over cheesecake; push pieces into batter, covering completely. Bake 50 to 55 minutes or until almost set.* Remove from oven to wire rack. With knife, loosen cake from side of pan; cool.

4 Cover; refrigerate. Just before serving, garnish as desired. Cover; refrigerate leftover cheesecake.

Cheesecakes are less likely to crack if baked in a water bath.

BEST BROWNIES

½ cup (1 stick) butter or margarine, melted

1 cup sugar

1 teaspoon vanilla extract

2 eggs

½ cup all-purpose flour

⅓ cup HERSHEY'®S Cocoa

¼ teaspoon baking powder

¼ teaspoon salt

Heat oven to 350°F. Grease 8- or 9-inch square baking pan. Stir butter, sugar and vanilla in bowl. Add eggs; beat well with spoon. Stir together flour, cocoa, baking powder and salt; gradually add to egg mixture, beating until well blended. Spread batter in prepared pan. Bake 20 to 25 minutes or until brownies begin to pull away from sides of pan. Cool completely in pan on wire rack.

Chocolate Crumb Crust: Heat oven to 350°F. Combine 1½ cups (about 45 wafers, crushed) vanilla wafer crumbs, 6 tablespoons powdered sugar, 6 tablespoons HERSHEY'®S Cocoa and 6 tablespoons butter or margarine (melted). Press crumb mixture onto bottom and ½ to 1 inch up side of 9-inch springform pan. Bake 8 minutes; cool slightly.

Acknowledgments

The publisher would like to thank the companies and organizations listed below for the use of their recipes and photographs in this publication.

California Walnut Board
Campbell Soup Company
Crystal Farms®
Dole Food Company, Inc.
Florida Department of Agriculture and Consumer Services, Bureau of Seafood and Aquaculture
The Hershey Company
McCormick®
Ortega®, A Division of B&G Foods North America, Inc.

METRIC CONVERSION CHART

VOLUME MEASUREMENTS (dry)

$1/8$ teaspoon = 0.5 mL
$1/4$ teaspoon = 1 mL
$1/2$ teaspoon = 2 mL
$3/4$ teaspoon = 4 mL
1 teaspoon = 5 mL
1 tablespoon = 15 mL
2 tablespoons = 30 mL
$1/4$ cup = 60 mL
$1/3$ cup = 75 mL
$1/2$ cup = 125 mL
$2/3$ cup = 150 mL
$3/4$ cup = 175 mL
1 cup = 250 mL
2 cups = 1 pint = 500 mL
3 cups = 750 mL
4 cups = 1 quart = 1 L

VOLUME MEASUREMENTS (fluid)

1 fluid ounce (2 tablespoons) = 30 mL
4 fluid ounces ($1/2$ cup) = 125 mL
8 fluid ounces (1 cup) = 250 mL
12 fluid ounces ($1\frac{1}{2}$ cups) = 375 mL
16 fluid ounces (2 cups) = 500 mL

WEIGHTS (mass)

$1/2$ ounce = 15 g
1 ounce = 30 g
3 ounces = 90 g
4 ounces = 120 g
8 ounces = 225 g
10 ounces = 285 g
12 ounces = 360 g
16 ounces = 1 pound = 450 g

DIMENSIONS

$1/16$ inch = 2 mm
$1/8$ inch = 3 mm
$1/4$ inch = 6 mm
$1/2$ inch = 1.5 cm
$3/4$ inch = 2 cm
1 inch = 2.5 cm

OVEN TEMPERATURES

250°F = 120°C
275°F = 140°C
300°F = 150°C
325°F = 160°C
350°F = 180°C
375°F = 190°C
400°F = 200°C
425°F = 220°C
450°F = 230°C

BAKING PAN SIZES

Utensil	Size in Inches/Quarts	Metric Volume	Size in Centimeters
Baking or Cake Pan (square or rectangular)	$8 \times 8 \times 2$	2 L	$20 \times 20 \times 5$
	$9 \times 9 \times 2$	2.5 L	$23 \times 23 \times 5$
	$12 \times 8 \times 2$	3 L	$30 \times 20 \times 5$
	$13 \times 9 \times 2$	3.5 L	$33 \times 23 \times 5$
Loaf Pan	$8 \times 4 \times 3$	1.5 L	$20 \times 10 \times 7$
	$9 \times 5 \times 3$	2 L	$23 \times 13 \times 7$
Round Layer Cake Pan	$8 \times 1\frac{1}{2}$	1.2 L	20×4
	$9 \times 1\frac{1}{2}$	1.5 L	23×4
Pie Plate	$8 \times 1\frac{1}{4}$	750 mL	20×3
	$9 \times 1\frac{1}{4}$	1 L	23×3
Baking Dish or Casserole	1 quart	1 L	—
	$1\frac{1}{2}$ quart	1.5 L	—
	2 quart	2 L	—